"This book will change how you think about creativity in business. Most of us believe marketing creativity is a risky hit-or-miss proposition. Fallon and Senn demonstrate that business creativity is a rigorous process with a tremendous upside if you get it right."

—Harvey Mackay, author,
*Swim with the Sharks
Without Being Eaten Alive*

"The advertising world will have to change to survive as people pay less and less attention to television advertisements. Pat Fallon and his world-famous agency grasped this; the techniques he pioneered and describes in *Juicing the Orange* will soon become standard industry practices."

—Faith Popcorn, Founder and CEO,
Faith Popcorn's BrainReserve

"*Juicing the Orange* may be the most interesting, enjoyable, and informative book on enhancing business performance available. The authors' humble, thoughtful delivery of a truly valuable message qualifies this book for my 'must read' rating."

—Kenneth J. Roering, Professor,
Marketing and Logistics Management,
Carlson School of Management,
University of Minnesota

"*Juicing the Orange* breaks the mold of a business how-to by providing the perfect metaphor for reconnecting people with their creativity. If any book can demystify creativity, this is it!"

—Richard J. Leider,
Founder, The Inventure Group;
author, *The Power of Purpose*;
and coauthor, *Repacking Your Bags*

Juicing the Orange

Juicing the Orange

How to Turn Creativity

Pat Fallon and Fred Senn

Harvard Business School Press • Boston, Massachusetts

into a Powerful Business Advantage

[Library of Congress Cataloging-in-Publication Data

Fallon, Pat.
 Juicing the orange : lessons in using creativity as a competitive marketing advantage / Pat Fallon and Fred Senn.
    p. cm.
 ISBN 1-59139-927-0
1. Marketing. 2. Creative ability in business. 3. Product management. I. Senn, Fred. II. Title.
 HF5415.F27 2006
 658.8'02—dc22

                    2005036310

Contents

Acknowledgments

The inspiration, and much of the raw material for this book, comes from our entries in the EFFIEs, an annual competition sponsored by the New York American Marketing Association, which bestows awards for advertising effectiveness. We're grateful to the New York AMA for championing this competition. The EFFIEs hold our feet to the fire and force our industry to be more accountable to the bottom line. They are a great way to celebrate creativity that works.

These EFFIE cases were created by our people on the firing line—those who do the research, distill the strategies, create the work, and make sure it gets to market. These are people who go above and beyond the call of duty, who love to make marketing history. This book is about what they do so well; we hope it tells their story as it deserves to be told. They are our heroes, and we are immensely proud of them.

We thank our clients. The joy of our business is in bringing something to market for smart and brave clients, and then watching it work. One of the hidden benefits is that we get to learn from our clients. They are our best teachers, and they have often become our dear friends outside work. Pat McGuiness, president of Nestlé Purina PetCare, has been our client for sixteen years. He taught us how to harness our brand of creativity to get real results in the world of packaged goods. Several have given us an opportunity to work with them in a second business life: Jim McDowell at Porsche and BMW; Dick Brown at Ameritech and EDS; Jerry Dow first at United Airlines and now at Vanguard Car Rental (National and Alamo); Chris Hawken at Skoda and then at Volkswagen in Asia; and Amy Wilkins at the Children's Defense Fund and then the Trust for Early Education. These are business partners who have shaped our enterprise.

We were encouraged to charge ahead with this project by the people at Harvard Business School Press, even though an advertising agency is not their natural source of material. But they have been supportive and patient as they came face-to-face with an unfamiliar form of right-brain capitalism. Executive Editor Kirsten Sandberg has been relentless: "More clarity—less exaggeration, boys." Kirsten is a cheerleader with a whip. We needed her brand of tough love to make this book happen. Marcy Barnes-Henrie, Senior Production Goddess, and copyeditor Betsy Hardinger forced us to use language that would make our mothers proud in spite of our attempts to write the way we talk. Thank you to Ralph Fowler for the refreshing interior design. Thanks, too, to the rest of the Press team involved in packaging and promoting the book, namely Dino Malvone, Julia Ely, Mark Bloomfield, Erin Brown, Todd Berman, Mike Fender, Zeenat Potia, Hollis Heimbouch, and David Goehring.

The task of writing this book was made almost bearable because of the support of our friend in the book business: our agent John Larson. Without his coaching, we would still be talking about writing a book someday.

Here in Minneapolis, awards for bravery go to Kim Eskro, our administrative assistant for more than a decade, who had to keep track of the countless versions, ads, charts, deadlines, and mood swings of two first-time authors with full-time day jobs. The unflappable Susan Flynn, our library director, amazed us with her ability to hunt down two decades' worth of industry facts in nanoseconds, and then do it again when we lost her first note.

The twenty-fifth anniversary we are marking with this book gives us pause. We consider ourselves extremely fortunate to be in this business with the wonderful people we work with every day. That's where the joy is. To them, we say, thank you!

Chapter One

Redefining Creativity in Today's Marketing Environment

In 1980, when we first contemplated starting our own agency, the advertising world was buzzing about something called "media leverage." Instead of purchasing airtime and magazine space strategically, marketers sought media leverage, or media clout, by buying up as much of both as possible in an effort to drown out the competition. Even though research showed that people develop a psychological resistance to repeated exposure to a single ad, Madison Avenue was bombarding consumers and calling it success.

To us, the advertising industry was spending itself into irrelevance, and so we saw an opportunity. With Tom McElligott, Irv Fish, and Nancy Rice, we founded Fallon McElligott Rice (now Fallon Worldwide) in 1981. We imagined a new kind of agency that would communicate with consumers in fresh, intelligent, and engaging ways, so that our clients wouldn't have to shout ten times to be heard once.

In the course of many late-night planning meetings, we wrote down what we believed. These ideals—which still govern our day-to-day business—included statements such as "the belief in family as a business model," "the necessity of having fun," and "seeing risk taking as a friend," but the following tenet headed the list: "the single-minded devotion to, and the belief in, the power of creativity."

Publicly announcing our devotion to creativity put us in risky territory. In the world of marketing communications, "creative" typically means "self-indulgent," the kind of *art for art's sake* ads that win awards but don't affect a client's bottom line. In the larger business world, *creativity* can be an even more pejorative word. Innovation is prized, but creativity conjures images of an improv group brought in for a team-building exercise, or empty exhortations to "think outside the box."

We thought of creativity in terms of the great creative work of the golden age of advertising in the 1960s, when ad agency legends such as David Ogilvy (of Ogilvy & Mather) and Bill Bernbach (of Doyle Dane Bernbach) revolutionized marketing communications by demonstrating that creativity could deliver a client's desired results. We believed—and still believe—that business should hold creativity to this higher standard. Imagination is the last legal means of gaining an unfair advantage over the competition.

Our goal was to help our clients outsmart rather than outspend their competitors, to leverage brains over budgets, to juice the orange rather than drain our clients' wallets. We labeled this fledgling idea *creative leverage,* the daily practice of

A NEW ADVERTISING AGENCY FOR COMPANIES THAT WOULD RATHER OUTSMART THE COMPETITION THAN OUTSPEND THEM.

Left to right: Fred Senn, Account Service. Nancy Rice, Executive Art Director. Pat Fallon, President. Tom McElligott, Creative Director. Irv Fish, Treasurer.

> "I know that only about half of my advertising works. The trouble is, I don't know which half."
> John Wanamaker

If you're spending money on advertising, you've probably wondered: Is anybody out there listening?

The answer to that question may come as a shock.

Consider the following facts: American business will spend over $54 billion on advertising this year. According to one estimate cited in *The Journal of Advertising Research*, that money will buy over 200 thousand messages per person, or approximately 560 messages every day for every man, woman and child in America.

Of those 560 messages, the average person will notice only 76.

Of those 76, only 12 will be remembered.

And of those 12, 3 will be remembered negatively.

From 560 to 76 to 12 to 9 — *an attrition rate of more than 98%!*

Sobering, isn't it?

But the news gets worse before it gets better.

THE CLUTTER TRAP.

In an effort to counteract the dwindling effectiveness of their messages, more and more companies increase their media frequency. This leads to clutter.

Advertisers like Wisk and Sanka, once content to run their shrill, tedious commercials several times a week, now may run them several times an hour, trying to bore their way into the consumer's consciousness.

Ironically, while the number of messages (and media costs) have doubled in the past several years, consumers now pay less attention than ever before.

In fact, a growing body of evidence suggests that increased frequency may actually be self-defeating.

In 1976, *The Harvard Business Review* warned,

> "Heavy media spending can even work against you.... repeated exposure to an advertisement may give rise to what psychologists label 'perceptual defense', to irritation, or even to outright rejection."

RAISING AWARENESS, NOT BUDGETS.

It's clear that if you want your message to be one of the precious few that are remembered — the less than 2% — you've got your work cut out for you.

Outspending the competition is increasingly expensive and, as we've seen, may even work against you.

Instead of trying to *outspend* the competition, why not try to *out-think* them? With messages so interesting that even the most indifferent consumer will stop and look.

According to researcher Daniel Starch, one advertisement can outperform another advertisement for the same product in the same media at the same time by 500%.

Obviously, the preferred way to improve effectiveness is not to increase the *spending level* of your advertising, but to increase the *interest level* of your advertising.

SCARCITY OF IMAGINATION.

Unfortunately, raising the interest level of your advertising is easier said than done. The creative imagination to make great advertising — advertising that builds bridges between products and customers — is rare.

As *The Harvard Business Review* once observed,

> "...creativity is like peace. Everybody wants it, everyone seems to have some ideas about it, but nobody seems able to produce it."

Once every several years, however, an advertising agency with the ability to produce truly exciting, original and compelling advertising appears. Fallon McElligott Rice is such an agency.

Although we've just opened our doors, the campaigns we've created at past agencies are famous. They've won market share for our clients, and a lion's share of awards for us. They've been studied in journalism schools, and copied by competitors.

In every case, these campaigns *seemed* like they had more money behind them than they did. The ideas were big; the budgets small.

WHAT WE BELIEVE.

At Fallon McElligott Rice we believe in advertising the way Ray Rubicam, Leo Burnett, David Ogilvy and Bill Bernbach once practiced it.

We believe that imagination is one of the last remaining legal means you have to gain an unfair advantage over your competition.

We believe you shouldn't have to repeat yourself ten times to be heard once.

We believe there is no such thing as a "me-too"product,only "me-too"advertising. And we believe that great advertising is, has been, and always will be created in full partnership with great clients.

If you're beginning to have some questions about whether anybody out there is listening to *your* advertising, perhaps you should talk to us. Soon.

We have a lot of ideas, a lot of energy, and a lot to prove.

FALLON McELLIGOTT RICE
89 South 9th Street, Minneapolis, Minnesota 55402   Telephone 612-332-2445

Our opening ad, July 20, 1981. This manifesto has an almost absurd amount of copy, but we felt it was essential to articulate our vision. Twenty-five years later, the statistics are worse, and globalization and technology have changed the marketing environment, but the solution is the same: applied creativity.

making creativity actionable and accountable for changing consumer behavior.

Creative leverage combines the thoroughness of the left brain and the artistry of the right. It means spurning convention, taking risks, and questing for human truths while researching rigorously, and executing boldly. Creative leverage happens at every phase in the development and execution of a marketing campaign. It also happens in every job, not just the ones traditionally associated with creativity, such as art directors and copywriters.

The First Test Case of Creative Leverage

Our very first client was a local barbershop with an unwieldy name: 7 South 8th for Hair. The shop could afford only some small advertisements in the downtown shopper and a few posters at nearby bus shelters. The owners had no money for production. Zero. We had to develop an advertising campaign without the usual conventions of the category: no hair models, no stylists, not even a photographer.

So we did the opposite of the beautiful fashion ad. We featured pictures of famous people with bad haircuts.

Over that famous photo of a disheveled Albert Einstein, we put the headline, "A bad haircut can make anyone look dumb," and over a picture of the Susan B. Anthony dollar, "A bad haircut can take you out of circulation." We did twisted takes on Richard Nixon, Betty Boop, and others whose bad haircuts everybody recognized. The barbershop's target market loved the campaign so much that people were stealing the posters from bus stops.

A bad haircut is no
laughing matter.
7 South 8th for Hair
804 LaSalle Avenue / Call 333-1376 for appointment

Bowl cut. This campaign didn't have the rigorous strategic component of true creative leverage, but using Moe Howard as the poster boy for a hair salon was certainly a big idea.

At first blush, the ads for 7 South 8th are merely attention getting, but the seeds of true creative leverage are there. Mick Freund, one of the owners of the salon, was a risk taker with an irreverent and playful sense of humor, and so the ads fit his personality and infused meaning into an otherwise plain-sounding and forgettable address.

Moreover, the campaign's running joke was based on an emotional truth: everyone can relate to the everyday humiliation of getting a bad haircut. More important, the campaign got results. In its first month, revenues were up 62 percent over the preceding month, and 68 percent over same month of the preceding year. After that, the salon enjoyed double-digit growth for the next fourteen months—all thanks to creativity, not cash.

Consider the carefully tracked world of packaged goods. Nestlé Purina, a client of ours, suffered from a common problem facing many companies: commoditization of its category and the loss of traction by Purina Dog Chow, its primary brand. In 1994, sales were slipping. Thanks to a growing array of new premium brands, consumers had many more brand choices. Specialty pet stores and big box retail had opened up new channels of distribution outside the supermarket, a traditional Purina stronghold. Even people who trusted the brand were buying it far less frequently.

You wouldn't think that there was much room for fresh thinking in dog food advertising. The USDA required that all pet food be nutritionally complete and balanced, and that made it difficult to substantially differentiate a product based on features and benefits. Meanwhile the advertising conventions of the category were well established. You could almost write your own dog food ad in your head: a bounding golden retriever with a lustrous coat frolics with her loving, happy family. A kindly veterinarian in a white lab coat puts in a cameo, lending nutritional credibility. At the end, everyone's tail is wagging.

An account planner at an advertising agency is responsible for interpreting the market, understanding the customer, and tracking the trends that shape the category. Our account planners are expected to be creative in their approach to consumer learning, an especially challenging task—because of the legislated limitations of the category. As they pored over all the existing research and tracking studies they reached two significant conclusions. First, there were no problems with the Purina brand; it enjoyed nearly universal trust among pet owners. Second, Purina didn't necessarily need to find new customers; many people were simply buying Dog Chow less often. But we didn't yet understand why.

In the case of Purina, the planning team initially did what creative people often do when the status quo frustrates them: they threw out all their assumptions about what a dog food brand could mean to consumers. They started from scratch. Instead of conducting impersonal telephone surveys during dinnertime, the planners tapped their own network of dog-owning friends, spending long hours in people's homes watching interactions between families and their pets. The goal was to uncover what really drove a dog owner's buying choice.

They discovered something remarkable: that they could divide the world into two groups. The first group fed their pets a steady diet of one brand of dog food. This group included breeders, hunters, and trainers, who knew that veterinarians recommended that dogs receive a steady diet. Despite their image as four-legged garbage disposals, dogs actually have very sensitive stomachs. The second group of owners treated their dogs as family members. Figuring that dogs were like people and thus craved variety, people in this group picked a different bag of food every time they went to the store. Anthropomorphism, and not what was best for the dog, drove purchase patterns.

The team tested this idea and quickly found something interesting: when people learned that a steady diet was better for their dog, they naturally stopped sampling and bought only one brand. Because they knew and trusted the Purina brand, in many cases they bought Dog Chow.

This simple but compelling insight drove the *creative brief*—the tightly written situation analysis that provides direction to creative and media teams: "Parents like to feed a variety of foods to their kids. Dog owners often feel the same way about their pets. But they shouldn't. Feeding variety can be harmful to a dog's digestive system. The best way to ensure your dog has a healthier, happier life is to feed a consistent diet of Purina Dog Chow every day."

For the next two years, we ran advertising on that simple message. The campaign was humorous and attention getting but never strayed from the essential truth: a consistent diet is healthier for your dog.

The results for Purina were remarkable. By focusing the Dog Chow message entirely on educating consumers on a single, simple truth (known by all veterinarians, breeders, and trainers), the campaign turned Purina's business losses into gains. One thought, well expressed, reversed a downward trend and drove double-digit growth in a low-interest commoditized category. In the first two years of the campaign, sales grew 12 percent each year. That's forty-five tons of dog food, contributing $35 million in additional revenue with no change in pricing or distribution.[1] The only thing we changed was the buying habits of Purina customers.

This is what we mean by juicing the orange.

Constantly switching your dog's food
can lead to finicky eating.

It's natural to think your dog wants variety. But by constantly switching his food, you could be training him to be a finicky eater. The fact is, a consistent diet of one nutritious food is actually healthier for dogs. That's why you can feel good about feeding your dog Purina® Dog Chow® brand dog food every day. With all the taste and nutrition dogs need. To make those bad eating habits disappear.

Purina® Dog Chow® Every Day.

Good boy.   Purina turned a sales decline into a double-digit sales gain by teaching people that feeding a variety of foods can be harmful to a dog's digestive system.

Putting Creative Leverage to Work

Pundits have written advertising's obituary, and we don't entirely disagree. As the cost of reaching households during prime-time television has risen (from $7.64 per thousand in 1994 to $19.85 per thousand in 2004), its impact has shrunk dramatically.[2] In 1965, 34 percent of adult evening viewers were able to name a brand advertised on a show they had watched the night before. By 2000, that number had dropped to 9 percent.[3] Not surprisingly, most marketers complain that they are spending more money to reach fewer people.

So what place does a traditional advertising agency have in this new world? When 90 percent of the population owns some type of device that delivers programming on demand and limits their exposure to commercial messages, 57 percent have signed up for the National Do Not Call Registry, and 20 percent have ad-blocking software on their personal computers, why bother with a traditional mass-marketing effort?[4] When Forrester Research, in a report pointedly titled "The Consumer Ad Backlash Worsens," notes that 52 percent of Americans say ads make it harder to "enjoy what I'm watching or reading," you can easily question your reason for being.[5]

Part of the answer lies in doing unconventional marketing using unconventional channels, but we argue that the answer is more fundamental than that. As the stories in this book demonstrate, communication in every medium, old and new (even the much-maligned Super Bowl spot), can be tremendously effective if the work is backed up by insightful research, rigorous strategy, and the right execution. This is where creative leverage comes in and gives you the tools you need to reach consumers who don't want to be reached, and to do it in a way that delights rather than annoys.

Creative leverage started as a reaction to media leverage, but over the years it's evolved into something more essential. It's hard to define and even harder to express as a best practice. But over the past twenty-five years, these seven guiding principles have helped us increase our success rate in solving marketing and branding problems. Although it's not a step-by-step process, these principles can get you started in juicing the orange.

The Seven Principles of Creative Leverage

1. Always start from scratch.

2. Demand a ruthlessly simple definition of the business problem.

3. Discover a proprietary emotion.

4. Focus on the size of the idea, not the size of the budget.

5. Seek out strategic risks.

6. Collaborate or perish.

7. Listen hard to your customers (then listen some more).

Always Start from Scratch

As we learned from the Purina campaign, we often gain more by taking a deep breath and rethinking a marketing problem from the beginning. Consider this: during World War II, military researchers in England carefully charted the damage to Allied planes returning from bombing runs over Germany. Statistically, the tail sections were the most heavily damaged, so the order went out to reinforce the tails. But the team was solving the wrong problem. Because the research focused only on the planes that returned, the researchers were blind to what was happening to the planes that were shot down. Once they deduced that the lost planes must have suffered damage to the fuselage or wings, they were able to take effective action.

If you don't start from scratch, you could get stuck in the mind-sets of those who went before you.

Demand a Ruthlessly Simple Definition of the Business Problem

In the 1992 presidential campaign, James Carville put a sign on the wall at Clinton campaign headquarters: "It's the economy, stupid." It never became an official talking point or the tagline for a TV spot, but this problem definition guided the campaign's strategy by focusing on the voters' greatest concern that summer.

In the language of poets, we're talking about "the one given line." At Fallon we call this "relentless reductionism." In a marketplace where real product differences can be hard to find, much less communicate, simplifying the marketing problem is essential. In Fallon's training program, our account executives learn 127 specific questions in three fields of interrogation to find the *one* consumer insight that forms the basis for the solution. Go to www.juicingtheorange.com to see this list of questions we use to guide our situation analysis.

Discover a Proprietary Emotion

In his book *How Customers Think,* Gerald Zaltman—a Harvard Business School professor and a fellow at Harvard's Mind, Brain and Behavior Institute—shows how marketers can learn from the science of how our brains work. Zaltman points out that market research is often conducted as if decisions come from pure logic, with emotion playing only a bit part. As it turns out, our emotions play a crucial role in coding, storing, and retrieving memories, which in turn form the foundation of decision making. "If the idea doesn't have emotional significance for us," Zaltman writes, "we're not likely to store it, and therefore it won't be available for later recall."[6]

Marketers who favor reason over emotion will find themselves quite literally forgotten. That's why we push to discover what we call a proprietary emotion. We first examine the category for any thread of emotion that the competition has underleveraged or overlooked. Then it's time for the preemptive strike—a bold and engaging message that connects our client's brand to how people live their lives. By the time competition catches up to the insight, our client already owns the territory.

Focus on the Size of the Idea, Not the Size of the Budget

Unlike scotch or beer, vodka once was a blank slate in terms of having a product image. Then in 1981, TBWA ran its first Absolut ad in *The New Yorker.* There were no product claims about taste or smoothness, only the mystique created around the unmistakable silhouette of the Absolut bottle. In the absence of meaningful product differences, this brand grew to dominate its category on the strength of its advertising, and more specifically on the strength of the idea TBWA created in the consumer's mind.

The Absolut campaign was creative leverage through design. With nothing more than the shape of the bottle and some clever wordplay, Absolut invited people to participate in an evolving visual story. What could be better than having your audience wonder where you were going to take this next?

When this campaign launched in 1981, Absolut shipments were a little more than a hundred thousand liters a year. By 1989, they stood at 29 million liters, and a decade later they reached more than 58 million liters.[7] All the super-premium vodkas that have come out since owe their success to Absolut.

Seek Out Strategic Risks

In 1990, General Motors launched its new Saturn car company to compete with Japanese compacts, but aside from workmanlike quality, not much in Saturn's design or engineering warranted America's attention. Ad agency Hal Riney, however, discovered during its market research that people were not interested in yet another new American car. What they wanted was a different car buying experience.

Today, the notion of "A Different Kind of Car Company" seems logical and intuitive, but GM and Saturn took a risk in basing their branding not on the car but on a radically rethought relationship between buyers and dealers. This brand position required the total commitment of employees, dealers, and salespeople (and they pulled it off gallantly), but we argue that the real risk would have been for GM to ignore the emotional truth that Riney's planners had uncovered. (But then, after its initial success, Saturn marketers began to neglect this advantage they had created. They now sound like everyone else. What a pity.) As marketing problems become more complex, creative leverage demands a higher tolerance for risk. If you don't take risks, your competitors will.

Collaborate or Perish

On April 19, 2005, when the U.S. government released new dietary guidelines, two smart "marketeering" teams in the Pepsi portfolio were ready. The day the announcement made headlines in the press, Quaker Oats and Tropicana Orange Juice collaborated to run a half-page ad with the banner, "Get half your daily fruit and whole grains before you're even out of your slippers." Clearly, media, PR, and advertising people in two separate companies got more bang for the buck by collaborating on the joint ad and timing their message perfectly.

Collaboration isn't a choice anymore; the question is how good you can be at it. For many years, Robert Kelley of Carnegie Mellon University has been asking people at a wide variety of companies the same question: "What percentage of the knowledge you need to do your job is stored in your own mind?" In 1986, the answer was typically about 75 percent, but by 1997, the portion had slid to 15 to 20 percent.[8]

Listen Hard to Your Customers (Then Listen Some More)

The only way we know out of the commodity trap, is to listen to your customers so you can improve the value proposition without lowering the price. Big box consumer electronic retailer Best Buy, for example, looked at the competition and didn't like what they saw. Wal-Mart made it tough to compete on price, while Amazon.com had a head start on the convenience of online shopping.

So, Best Buy went out and talked to customers to find out what kind of shopping experience people wanted when they were looking for consumer electronics. They went further and did "shop-alongs" where researchers acted like anthropologists observing a foreign culture. They asked what they could do better.

The market researchers listened to customers in both their own stores and their competitors' and found five different segments, each with its own information needs and shopping preferences. Best Buy then revamped their entire operation to serve those five segments in distinctly different environments.

for example, Best Buy is exploring their understanding of the kind of shopping experience and technical support a soccer mom is looking for. It's starting to pay off. In 2005, the pilot stores had twice the growth rate as their old model stores.[9]

Consumers have never been smarter about marketing than they are now. If you engage them early enough in the research process and ask them the right questions, then you'll never be far from figuring out how best to connect with them.

A Cautionary Tale in Art for Art's Sake

When we've misfired, inevitably it was because we overlooked one or more of these principles. For example, in 1998, Miller Brewing Company hired us to help its struggling Miller Lite brand. Miller Lite was not winning blind taste tests against Bud Light. Also, Miller Lite was outspent and outmuscled by Budweiser's superior distribution system. Sales were falling and the brand was in trouble.

We started our business with the dream of solving this kind of marketing problem: big category, lots of national exposure, a seemingly insurmountable problem. Where others had failed, we'd come riding to the rescue.

Our diagnosis was that the Miller Lite brand had lost its way. It didn't have enough personality. The brand lacked an edge. Miller agreed. To chip away at Budweiser's dominance, we created a campaign that distinguished Miller from Bud by giving Miller a distinctive, irreverent personality that would appeal to Generation X's love of irony and absurdity.

We found that the long-abandoned concept of "Miller time" still had resonance. Our target demographic of young adult males embraced "Miller time" even though they were unclear about what it meant. We would redefine "Miller time." They also told us that a beer drinker's best moments often were spontaneous and unplanned, thus the insight, "At Miller Time, anything can happen."

Over the next three years we created more than one hundred fifty TV spots and print ads. Some were damn funny. In one of the most popular spots, a guy dances the twist in front of a bottle of Miller Lite after reading the instructions, "Twist to Open." But we went too far. Many of the spots were weird for weird's sake. Some looked like clips from a Czechoslovakian student film festival. In July of 1997, *Brandweek* wrote, "Perhaps one of the brashest repositioning to come down the ad pike has been the Miller Time campaign that boasts a series of irreverent, even sophomoric ads from 'creative superstar Dick' that have established a demographic fault line in TV Land, drawing favorable reviews from audiences under 34 and nearly universal pans elsewhere."[10]

There were two deeper problems than how our ads were received. First, we forgot about the beer. More importantly, in our analysis of Miller's business problem, we had left out a key component of any beer company's success: the distributors. Miller's distributors were a generation older than our target market and had witnessed the rise of Miller Lite a decade earlier during the strategically sound, but repetitive campaign of old athletes yelling, "Tastes great! Less filling!" The distributors lacked patience for our experiment and were frankly alienated by spots like the one featuring a guy in a beaver suit attacking a log cabin.

Without the distributors' support and lacking clear strategic integrity behind the wackiness, our work for Miller Lite

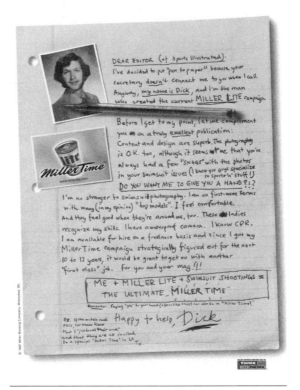

"Dear Editor." This ad ran in *Sports Illustrated.* We thought
it was pretty funny at the time, but a lack of guiding strategy
and a lack of alignment with the distributors kept the campaign
from making an impact on Miller's business.

became the poster child for creativity run amok. Clearly we
had failed to deliver on some of our key principles.

What to Expect from This Book

In the past twenty-five years, we've had more hits than misses.
We're not a huge agency—we rank twenty-eighth nationwide
and have five hundred employees worldwide—but we take
pride in delivering what our clients need. Over the years, in

addition to the companies mentioned in this book, we've been fortunate to have worked with clients like the *Wall Street Journal,* Federal Express, Porsche, Prudential Insurance Company, Nikon, QUALCOMM, Nuveen Investments, Starbucks, Microsoft, Georgia Pacific, BBC, Kitchen Aid, Saint Paul Travelers Insurance, and NBC.

We've written this book to explain how creative leverage can guide you in solving marketing and branding problems. The ten stories we tell here explore creative leverage from every angle. We've chosen clients from our twenty-five-year history that could not differ more: an airline on the ropes, a blue jeans company with an unfashionable image, a maverick cell phone company, an obsolescing high-tech behemoth, a bank that wanted to be unbanklike, and a famous tourist destination that no one really knew about. Along the way, we riff on magazines, luxury cars, an electronic stock exchange, and others.

Many of these campaigns have been written about in the national press and the trades, and some have even been taught in MBA programs across the country. We'll take you behind the scenes. You'll see the impasses and the breakthroughs, the calculated risks and the fruits of high-level collaboration. Each case is a lesson in applying creative leverage. You'll see why Lee Jeans pegged its future in men's jeans on a ceramic doll from the 1930s; why BMW gave up its TV budget to produce short films for the Internet; and how business-to-business marketer EDS pulled the trigger on a $3 million Super Bowl spot even though Super Bowl advertising is an enormous gamble even for consumer products.

At the end of each story, we'll talk about the business results. Because clients differ in the way they define measurable

Creative Leverage on the Web

We have a special place on our Web site where you can see the television spots or video we refer to in the cases. Go to www.juicingtheorange.com and click on "See the Work."

results, we do our best to put our role in its proper business context. The ultimate metric for creative leverage is revenues that lead to profitable growth, but our clients have also had other goals, such as improved public opinion, heightened awareness, greater purchase intent, or even an uptick in stock price.

Given the sorry state of advertising's return on investment, you have every right to be skeptical about whether creativity works. We are not proposing that the creative leverage presented in these stories will restructure business models, but we hope to show the impact on the bottom line when it came to solving marketing and branding problems. We'll present the evidence as best we can and let you decide.

Chapter 10 is about the importance of culture in fostering creativity. We believe that you have more creativity in your organization than you realize, and we believe that you can find it, develop it, and use it more effectively. We also hope to dispel myths about creativity, which unfortunately carries a lot of negative baggage in the business world. In 1997, *California Management Review* published a study that investigated how experts in fields ranging from physics to art to business felt about such abstract concepts as wisdom, intelligence, and creativity. "In most fields there was little or no relationship between behaviors believed to characterize the wise person," the authors of the study wrote, "but in the business group, the relation [to creativity] was actually negative: Businesspeople tended to believe that it was unwise to be creative."[11]

By the time you reach the end of the book, we think you'll agree that it's unwise to be any other way.

Chapter Two

Outpacing the Commoditization of Your Brand

At one time or another, most ad agencies have had a bank client—we've had at least four—and the natural tendency of a typical bank client is to be conservative. The conventional wisdom is that people choose a bank based on purely rational criteria such as location and charges for ATM use and other services, and these assumptions lead to a "rates and fees" approach to marketing. When banks do attempt branding work, they typically operate on a narrow emotional bandwidth—friendly, neighborly, or trustworthy—but few have exhibited a genuine personality, or the willingness to commit to a sustained branding effort.

When Citibank gave us the opportunity to compete for its business in 1999, it wanted to take a different approach to both banking and brand management. Thanks to a radical transformation in the industry, this new approach was almost a necessity because there were new forces from outside the banking category threatening the cozy status quo. In the 1990s, there had been massive consolidation. From 1990 to 1998, more than four thousand banks merged in the United States, reducing the number in operation by 30 percent.[1]

Second, recent legislation had increased the number of services that banks could offer. Whereas banking was once a local concern, now megabanks could compete nationally and offer a broader range of products. Furthermore, the new regulations stopped protecting banks from the competitive forces of the marketplace. Players like General Electric, Microsoft, and the carmakers were offering credit card and consumer lending services.

Complicating matters, the category was reaching full commodity status. Banks had become the utilities of the financial world. With parity in product and distribution, not only did people not care about banks, but many people also didn't care which bank they used. Even Citi's credit card business lacked traction. Because its cards were often cobranded with another institution, only 25 percent of Citi's own cardholders realized that their card carried the Citi brand.

To thrive, Citi would have to find a credible and relevant reason for customers to choose Citi. In other words, they'd have to juice the orange and use creativity to forge a competitive advantage.

At Citi, Anne MacDonald, chief marketing officer, global consumer group, and Brad Jakeman, managing director of global marketing, faced these realities and hatched an audacious plan: to transform Citi into a global power brand, preeminent not only in financial services but also among other great consumer brands like Disney, Nike, or Coca-Cola. The new marketing team understood that brands like Nike have stability and momentum that increase their chance for long-term global growth.

Before addressing their brand's image, the executives at Citi first made key organizational changes aimed at becoming more customer-centric in everything they did. They beefed up the quality of customer service at all touch points and added more consumer-friendly products, such as identity theft protection for Citi-issued credit cards. But the most daring part of the plan was the way the executives wanted to position their brand. Even though they didn't fully know what the term meant, MacDonald and Jakeman wanted to make Citi the world's first "unbanklike" bank.

Listen to Your Barber

Clients normally come to us thinking inside the confines of their own category. They want the world to see them as the best insurance company or the best car company or the most recognized fast food company. When Citibank looked at the brand image of financial services companies, it observed that its brand image was weak compared with its footprint in American business. Citibank wanted to stretch the boundaries. But banks didn't generate a lot of goodwill with the public. The executives understood that the way people viewed banks was too limiting for Citi's aspirations. This idea was at the heart of its desire to be unbanklike.

We found this idea liberating, and daunting. But we were grateful to be invited to pitch because we could sense that they meant what they said. Still, we were only one of many strong agencies competing for the account. The trade press even quoted Brad Jakeman as saying that he was smitten by Lee Clow, the legendary creative chief at Chiat\Day. We couldn't let that go. So we created a little gauge that could point left or right, with Lee Clow on one side and Pat Fallon on the other. We told the executives at Citi that we fully intended to move the "smitten" needle in our direction.

Before we started working on the concept of an unbank-like bank, we needed to understand Citibank's existing brand image. We also needed to understand Citi's customers better than any of our competitors did and in many ways even better than Citi itself. By interrogating their customer base, we hoped to find an essential truth that would link the two and help Citi deliver on its brand promise.

Citibank didn't have any baggage; for better or for worse it was an empty vessel. With the brand a blank slate, we focused on Citi's potential customers. A mass brand like Citi means a mass audience, specifically the mass of people ages twenty-five to fifty-nine with household incomes of $35,000 or more. In other words, just about everybody. We jumped on every piece of pertinent marketing research we could get our hands on, but the scale and scope of the target rendered much of the existing data useless.

So we started from scratch. Had Citi already been our client (as Purina had been), we would have camped out in its branches to observe customer behavior. But given the time crunch of a new business pitch, we instead put together a half-dozen exploratory focus groups. Focus groups have been maligned as an overused market research tool, a dull and misleading instrument. Some marketers believe that focus group respondents will tell you only what you want to hear. But we believed that our account planners could lead these focus groups in a way that uncovered the fresh insight that we needed.

Our planners listened hard, but this time around they weren't asking the right questions. We started getting the same answers, and they weren't very inspired ones. People talked blandly about peace of mind and security, interest rates, convenient locations, and ATM fees. Our creative team—hidden on the other side of a one-way mirror—was getting dross when it needed gold.

Our planners have learned to watch for a spike in energy in the room. Even when a focus group bad-mouths the product or the category, we listen because passion is often a better indicator of a potential insight than optimism. But these people didn't even fake interest. Our planners were desperate to find some emotional connection to the category, but the focus groups weren't even remotely interested in anything that had to do with banking.

Fortunately, one of our planners needed a haircut. While in the barber's seat, he agonized over the participants' lack of interest in banking. His barber set him straight: people don't care about banks, but they care a whole lot about money and its role in their lives.

How had we missed that? The problem was that we were looking at the customer's contact point with the bank rather than digging deeper into the reason they needed a bank in the first place. We were looking for a proprietary emotion in bank transactions rather than in a customer's relationship with their bank. Because we were leading the discussion, our bored respondents were happy to stay on script. In their minds, the gulf between the tedium of banking and the importance of money to their lives was so wide that the discussion couldn't ladder up to what really mattered.

We now saw that we needed to reframe the discussion in its entirety. Instead of talking about banks and money, we needed to get the participants talking about themselves. We tried another round of focus groups. This time, we got people talking about their lives and the role of money in them. We purposefully avoided the actual mechanics of banking. Immediately, our planners realized they were onto something. The energy in the room picked up. People were talking about money in terms of what made them happy, what they needed to live well. Suddenly, we had human beings, and not bank customers.

Even more remarkable was what these people were saying. These focus groups took place during the dot-com boom. According to the newspapers, everyone was obsessing with retiring by age forty. Start a company, take it public ASAP, and retire a millionaire. Or buy shares of an initial public offering, flip them a month later, and retire a millionaire. But the people in the second round of focus groups weren't talking about IPOs or Mercedes convertibles or vacations in the Seychelles. They saw money as a means, and little more. Being a millionaire wasn't a part of the fantasy.

Their words began to ring true, even though some of our team members were workaholics who couldn't imagine "getting by" as a financial goal. But we kept listening and watching. Over time, a pattern emerged. An entire new class of bank customers materialized. We labeled them "balance seekers," and we could already see how they might prefer an "unbanklike" bank.

In the spirit of simplifying the business problem, we reduced the solution to its essence: cultivate the balance seekers.

But Have We Discovered an Emotional Truth That Matters?

Unearthing an emotional truth is always an exhilarating starting point, but it is only a beginning. We can only imagine how the planners at Hal Riney felt when they identified those people who cared as much about how they bought a car as which car they bought and helped create the Saturn car company.

But before we got too excited, we needed to accomplish two goals. First, we had to verify the emotional truth; to win the account with these findings, we needed to establish the existence of this lost tribe of balance seekers beyond the focus group. How many were there? Would they be profitable bank customers? What kind of marketing messages would they respond to?

Second, we had to generate the big idea that would connect with these balance seekers. If there were no actionable way to help Citi connect with them, our insight about balance seekers would become interesting but useless.

So our planners dug deeper. Every week, omnibus research companies conduct telephone surveys across the nation with a large sample of people. When we need a quick read on a qualitative hunch, we turn to these firms for validation. For $1,000, you can buy a question in the survey, provided it's not product specific. We bought two. The first question was a qualifier to find out how many balance seekers were out there: "Thinking about attitudes of financial success, would you say financial success is having all the money you could ever want, or would you say it's having enough for basic necessities and a little left over to have fun?"

For those who answered it was having enough for the basics and a little left over we wanted to learn more about how they felt about this point of view toward money. Our second question was, "Would you say you have already achieved success, are not likely to ever achieve it, will achieve it in the future, or will always be working toward it?"

Almost half of the respondents (46 percent) said they were content having enough to get by; they were happy with their lives and would always be working toward success. This finding was hugely significant. Here was a large number of respondents with balance seeker tendencies that cut across all demographic lines of age, income, and education and yet hadn't shown up anywhere in the conventional research.

One of the indicators that we're on to an essential truth is that subsequent research keeps pointing back to the same place. Next, we tapped in to syndicated market research studies, the kind used by media planners everywhere, to further quantify the balance seeker target. Using questions that a large representative sample of Americans had already answered, we cross-referenced behaviors and attitudes about money and about life that confirmed that the balance seeker existed in great numbers. We were encouraged to find that about half of U.S. adults had strong balance seeking tendencies. Even better, these people indexed as having more assets and more bank accounts than the average bank customer.

This breakthrough was enormous. The team had verified and quantified a large group of people for whom money wasn't everything, and the number was large enough to justify our sharing it with Citibank. We didn't know how we were going to reach these balance seekers, but there was no question that they existed. We were halfway home.

Starting a Conversation with the Balance Seekers

Now that we had found this emotional truth, we had to propose how Citi could credibly own it and differentiate itself in the minds of its current and prospective customers. Before we could build a communications program, we needed to bring the balance seeker to life. Thus far, our work had been confined to research and number crunching. Now we had to capture the balance seeker in more human terms. We did an exercise we often do: based on the abstract characteristics we had identified, we imagined describing that person as our neighbor.

From this point on, the work took off. Instead of feeling as though we were writing ads, we felt we were connecting with this new audience. We had a mantra: "Citi understands there's more to life than money." In the brief, an account planner wrote, "These people want to live a rich life, not be rich." Our copywriter quickly reduced that to "Live richly."

The Balance Seeker: A Definition of Our Customer (circa 1999)

In this world of dot-com superstars, Powerball mania, and *Who Wants to Marry a Millionaire?*, Citi customers just smile and get on with their lives. In fact, they're kind of amused by the get-rich-quick mentality that seems to permeate the culture. They know what's achievable for them, and they're content with that. Sure, they'd like to have a little more money. Buy a nicer car or add a bedroom. Send their kids to a good school. Get that sixteen-foot bass boat. But they know that true financial success isn't some big pay date on a calendar in the future. It's not Ed McMahon knocking at the front door. True financial success lies in the little decisions they make every day regarding money. For them, money's not the goal. It's not what makes life worth living. Rather, money is the lubrication that keeps a happy life oiled and moving ahead. They measure success by the things they do, and not the money they amass. They actually understand that they can't have it all.

True financial success is a state of equilibrium. It's an intuitive feeling that they're using their money to get the most out of life today and tomorrow.

They're always trying to stay in that zone of equilibrium, but sometimes, as they say, sh*t happens. Things get out of whack. Life throws a curve. A roof needs to get fixed. An invitation to a party absolutely screams for a new dress. The car suddenly needs a complete brake job. And they must fight once again to find their new equilibrium. Nobody can do it for them; only *they* can regain balance.

They believe a bank is best qualified to help do this. But start talking "relationship," and they'll run the other way.

We then created some sample television ads. The spots showed real people doing things that mattered to them, things that brought them more joy than money ever would. The first spot was filmed in our assistant producer's back yard, with him spinning his young son like an airplane. There was no script, just these words appearing on the screen:

A sure way to get rich quick:
Count your blessings.
There's more to life than money.
There's a bank that understands that.
Citi. Live richly.

When it came time to pitch we were nervous. The idea we were advocating would surely put demands on the Citi organization in areas like training, leadership, and brand advocacy that go well beyond our role as marketers. The company's behavior would have to match the advertising, or else the entire construct would fall apart. As marketers, we could lead reality a bit—show the way, if you will—but we could not get too far out in front of the customer's actual experience or there would be a consumer backlash.

We anticipated some resistance and skepticism from Citi, but after we made our case, they were ready to bet the vault on it. They "got it" on a very human level. They could empathize with balance seekers, and they could see how they could serve this market better than anyone else. It was just the unbanklike approach that Citi was seeking—not only as an advertising campaign but also as an organizing approach to serving customers.

Big Ideas Have Broad Shoulders

We have produced more than 800 executions, including 175 in the well-known poster series that line the streets of Manhattan. The connection between the balance seeker and the brand took hold almost immediately. After the first eight-week flight of advertising, the tracking research showed that consumers' predisposition to use Citi as a financial services provider jumped 50 percent. Citi saw a 25 percent increase in Web site inquiries during that same advertising flight. Those early feel-good indicators proved to be no fluke. The campaign immediately started proving its ability to drive business. Credit card acquisition went up by 30 percent, home equity loan applications increased 14 percent, and small business card accounts rose 20 percent.[2]

Wall Street took notice. Analyst David Hilder of Bear Stearns wrote in a research report, "Citigroup did a good job of conveying the breadth of its global consumer franchise, especially a thoughtful and successful approach to consumer advertising, which is rare for a financial services company."[3] Citi was well on its way to establishing a solid position as a global power brand. By 2005, Citi had risen to twelfth place on Interbrand's list of the world's most valuable brands, the highest of any financial services company.[4]

The balance seeker also proved to be what we call a "platform idea." A platform idea can transcend advertising and touch on many aspects of a client's business. We felt that "Citibank knows there's more to life than money" was a brand philosophy that could apply to any number of Citibank product lines—in the credit card division, at the individual branches, or in the loan offices. If properly executed, a platform idea has the power to help transform the brand.

Practically every product fit under the "more to life than money" platform idea, and "Live richly" had the bandwidth to influence product development, retail branch design, billing statements, and virtually every contact point between Citi and its customers.

For example, as fear of identity theft swept the country, Citi introduced the best identity theft protection features available on any credit card. Rather than bland assurances, we did a series of arresting commercials where you see the victim of identity theft at home talking to the camera. But coming out of the victim's mouth is the voice of the criminal who stole his or her identity, gloating about all the purchases they'd made. The announcer concludes, "Citi identity theft solutions. Free with any Citi card. Help getting your life back? That's using your card wisely." The product features as well as the style of the commercials reinforced the "Live richly" theme.

Citibank also reinvigorated older products under the new brand identity. Citipro, a free financial planning service that provides an entry point for multiple retail product sales, had been in the market for some time, but after it was relaunched under the "Live richly" mantra, activity jumped. After the first six weeks, inquiries were up 67 percent, leading to a 184 percent increase in product sales.[5]

The best platform ideas can even work internally. We wrote a twenty-five-page booklet for Citi employees about how to identify and help customers who sought balance. We even created a job application to see whether future Citi bank employees could identify with the balance seeker ethos.

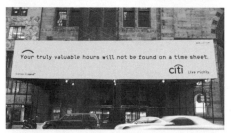

Citi on the streets. If it's unusual for a bank to connect on an emotional level, it's even more unusual for outdoor advertising to make an emotional connection. But who wouldn't smile and nod at these gems? There are now more than 175 executions of the "Live richly" theme, and they have even been published in a book.

The Balanced Seeker Travels Well

"Live richly" was originally conceived for the U.S. market. But the humanity of the concept is far more universal than we could have imagined. We have found balance seekers around the world, and the concept has translated well in Germany, Greece, Japan, and Brazil.

But there are subtle and important differences in these markets that have showed us the importance of continuing to listen to your customer even when you think you've got them figured out. As we extend the campaign geographically, the execution changes to match the cultural climate. Citi makes sure to approach the balance seekers in each country through the lens of their own culture rather than demanding global consistency.

The German balance seeker, for example, is concerned about security and health. The Greek balance seeker, on the other hand, cares about security but wants to live life to the fullest. A Greek consumer put it this way: "You can't have quality of life without security, but what's the point of being secure if it's no fun?"[6]

The Greek adaptation of the campaign is getting results. All expected measures of awareness and attitude have jumped, and net revenue from credit card operations is up 20 percent. The company received eleven thousand inbound calls during the loan promotion. High-interest savings accounts grew faster at participating branches than the combined growth of all products in the previous three years.[7]

Rigor and Creativity Will Get You Out of the Commodity Trap

This case started with a client that saw the dangers of the commodity trap and was committed to find a way to break out. They demanded to see something different. On our part, the account planners understood that satisfying the client's demands would take a level of insight that went beyond the norm.

When creative leverage works, there's a strategic breakthrough; you discover something about the target market that is new territory. The big lesson—and you'll see it in other stories as well—is that you've got to be relentless in your interrogation of the target market until you find this proprietary advantage. Lightbulbs don't go on until the house is wired right.

Chapter Three

Fighting for Your Brand's Voice

When we were offered the chance to bid on United Airlines' business in October 1996, the Chicago-based Leo Burnett ad agency had covered the business since the early 1960s. Thirty years before, Burnett had first invited travelers to "fly the friendly skies," and this elegant slogan was one of the most recognizable and enduring brand images for any of the legacy carriers. It conjured images of fresh, clean, gleaming planes and impeccable personal service, and it captured the fantasy of mobility and progress that formed the cornerstone of early commercial air travel.

The problem was that by the late 1990s the idea of flying friendly skies was obsolete. United was hearing from its regular customers that "friendly skies" meant little in today's harried and hassled world. Air travel had become part of the daily grind—a necessary evil—and not a symbol of freedom, much less accomplishment or prestige, and "friendly" was not even on the list of desired attributes. (Professional service, yes, but not friendly.) Over time, United's central brand claim had become irrelevant and, for some, even irritating.

We saw this as an opportunity for the airline to reconnect with consumers on a different basis, but, as with Citibank, we first needed to figure out which consumers we should target. To help us prepare for our pitch, United gave all the competing agencies a new study from Cambridge Research that analyzed the relationship between passenger segments and revenues. One fact jumped out at us: United got 48 percent of its revenues from 9 percent of its customers: frequent business travelers (FBTs) who flew United multiple times each month, often at the highest fares.

In cases like this deciding what not to do is as important as deciding what to do. Defining the business problem as simply as we could, we based our pitch on helping United connect with the FBTs to the exclusion of other segments, such as vacation travelers. The agency search committee was so intrigued by our relentless focus on the FBTs that we won its domestic business.[1] The win was an important one for us. At twenty-three hundred flights a day, United was the largest airline in the world. Every time we landed at Chicago's O'Hare airport and saw the rows upon rows of United tails, we pinched ourselves to think that we were United's advertising agency. (Ten years later, we still do.)

When we won this plum account—a profitable business in what was at the time a healthy category—we thought we'd be fine-tuning the airline's relationship with its most important customers. In 1996, the economy was still booming and there was no sign of the international turmoil to come. We never imagined the number and severity of the challenges that United would face over the next several years, nor how many important lessons we would learn about the importance of fighting for a brand's voice during a time of crisis.

Apology Needed

In the summer of 2000, just four years after we had won the account, both United and the industry found themselves in a new business climate. Labor and fuel costs and the airlines' pension structures were putting a strain on all the established national carriers. To make matters worse for United, its pilots were in a contract dispute. They weren't on strike, but they publicly refused to work overtime. As a result, United experienced an unprecedented number of flight delays and cancellations. Airports became campgrounds; United's consumers lost all patience; and its customer service desks were flooded with angry streams of stranded passengers.

United became the mascot for the problems of the industry as a whole. Despite years of deregulation, government officials were piling on, voicing their disappointment in United and promising new legislation to avoid such problems in the future. United pilots aired their frustrations with management on television. In short, it was both a business and public relations nightmare.

In such a crisis, a marketer's instinct is either to continue the campaign as if nothing were happening or to go silent until it blows over. Even though the company was in crisis, we thought that United's advertising could still serve the brand. Blurring the line between advertising and PR, we recommended a radical advertising concept: the public apology.

From the cabin of a United plane, chairman Jim Goodwin faced the camera in a paid announcement and apologized to United's customers. Here's the very straightforward message:

> *"Hello. I'm Jim Goodwin, chairman of United Airlines.*
>
> *"This summer, thousands of people had their travel plans disrupted while flying United Airlines. If you were one of them, I want to apologize personally on behalf of United.*
>
> *"To deal with the problem, we're reducing our flight schedule, so we don't make promises we can't keep.*
>
> *"As a leader, United has big plans down the road, but we're not going anywhere until we get you where you're going first."*

This wasn't your typical happy tune about the friendly skies, but it was absolutely necessary to stop the bleeding in the media and in the cash register. It did, with a positive, if temporary, effect. The announcement got positive news coverage on two hundred news outlets. Attitudinal measures such as repurchase intent jumped 8 percent. We saw a 12 percent jump in "United is my first choice airline." The business slide halted and even turned up a bit; there was a 2 percent increase in load, which equated to an 11 percent increase in yield because the business flyers were the ones coming back.[2]

What Do You Do in a National Crisis?

Then came 9/11. The tragedy, which shocked the world and crippled air travel around the globe, involved two United flights. The nation went into shock, and then into mourning. (Like everyone else in New York, our agency was reeling. Our New York office was on the twentieth floor of the Woolworth building on Broadway, and our people watched in horror from their office windows as people in the World Trade Center leaped to their deaths from the burning towers. Our building was temporarily condemned, and operations were moved out.)

Our immediate assignment from United: pull all advertising, and help us figure out how to respond. This was a hard moment. Our job was to be United's advertiser, but advertising was the last thing on anyone's mind. The whole idea of creating an ad that responded to this tragedy seemed inappropriate, but we had to do something even if, like the rest of America, we felt paralyzed.

All air traffic was grounded, and no one was sure when planes would fly again. Despite the barrage of government announcements and media coverage about people stranded at airports, we still weren't sure what United should say to the public. So, our account director and our account planner decided to talk to people at United—not the leaders but the people on the front lines.

They went out to the Minneapolis airport and with no agenda other than listening. What they found was a sense of solidarity that the account team hadn't seen before. United employees—the same ones that had just suffered through labor turmoil—were acting like an extended family. They all passionately and patriotically wanted to get the airline flying again, as soon as possible. The message they wanted to deliver to America was that they were determined to get United back as soon as possible to the business of getting passengers where they needed to go.

Inspired by the employees' sense of duty and allegiance to each other, our team leaders came back to the office and wrote a brief that went out to several teams on Friday afternoon, September 14. The heart of the brief was that the employees' unity was a moment worth capturing. For them to accomplish their mission of returning to normal, United employees needed to share their feelings with their customers and the rest of the country.

The next morning, a Saturday, one of our best writers sent in his response to the brief via fax. As we read his copy, we got goose bumps. We found ourselves nodding in complete agreement with its sentiment—not as marketers, but as citizens.

The ad ran nationwide on September 21, 2001. Creating this ad was an inflection point for our agency. We learned to take a client's crisis as our own, and we reconfirmed our belief in the importance of listening. The positive reaction from customers and employees alike let us know that we got it right.

Even Rougher Weather Ahead

On December 9, 2002, United Airlines filed for Chapter 11 debt protection. We were now dealing with the aftermath of 9/11 and the systemic effects of the tragedy on the airline industry. Needless to say, the lingering stigma of bankruptcy created its own special set of communication problems for United.

Our first task was to let all constituencies know that the enterprise was alive and competing. Second we needed to demonstrate that the company still had a sense of purpose and confidence. As management wrestled with pressing operational issues, our hope was to create solid marketing communications that would set the tone for the recovery.

Monday, September 10.

On Monday, a hose in my sink broke just when I needed to rush out the door, and I thought life was being unfair.

On Monday, when you ask people how they were doing, without much thought, or much contemplation, they replied "fine" or "good."

On Monday, the papers and the news magazines were filled with stories about the new fall TV schedule.

On Monday, there were not many people in the religious section at the bookstore.

On Monday, the American flag hung, for the most part, unnoticed at government buildings and at schools.

On Monday, we passed strangers without much regard.

On Tuesday, September 11, all that changed.

On Tuesday, September 11, different things seemed important.

On Tuesday, September 11, blissful naiveté was lost.
Sanctity was mercilessly shaken.

On Tuesday, September 11, somebody tried to take America apart.

On Tuesday, September 11, America came together.

On Tuesday, there were no Republicans, Democrats, yuppies, blue collars, or any other labels. There were only Americans.

On Tuesday, September 11, strangers died for each other.

On Tuesday, September 11, the best of the human spirit spit back into the eye of the worst.

On Tuesday, September 11, America was knocked to its knees.
On Tuesday, September 11, America got back up again.

We'd like to acknowledge the bravery and selflessness of the rescue workers, medical personnel, and extraordinary citizens of this country. Your acts of heroism and compassion have touched all our hearts. We'd also like to thank our employees for their caring professionalism in the wake of last week's horrible tragedy. We join you in mourning. As we join you in strength.

UNITED

United Airlines full-page newspaper ad, September 21, 2001. This was one of the most difficult ads we've ever had to write. The copy was inspired by listening to United employees, who needed to share their feelings with their customers and the rest of the country. A floor-to-ceiling version of this ad hangs just outside our conference room.

Enter Glenn Tilton, United's new CEO. In May 2003, Tilton brought in executive vice president of marketing John Tague, a forty-one-year-old who admitted to having "brand envy" of United when he had been the CEO of ATA. One of the first things Tague did was to tell us we were on notice: if our work didn't generate revenue, he'd look for a new agency.

We understood the urgency. People were flying again, but the bad news was that they weren't using the legacy carriers— United, Delta, Northwest Airlines, American Airlines, and US Airways. By 2003, the newer low cost carriers had already captured 20 percent of the market.[3] Passenger levels wouldn't return to their pre-9/11 levels for another two years.

In the summer of 2003, we launched three hard-sell retail promotions in an effort to leverage United's scale and create excitement. The good thing about this kind of activity is that you get instant feedback at the cash register. These three promotions added a billion dollars in incremental revenue to the struggling airline's coffers.[4] But these were unsustainable gains with little margin attached—we were selling seats at a discount. In order to reinvigorate the brand we would need to use creative leverage.

Unfortunately, United's Chapter 11 status left the company with little money to make tangible improvements or upgrades to the product. Furthermore, like all the other major airlines, United was completely commoditized. Indeed, research firm, Roper, found that more people see a difference worth paying for in cell phone plans than they do in airlines.[5] United's frequent flyer program was its most positive differentiator.[6] But the program was more of a defensive tool than an offensive weapon, keeping customers with United but not attracting new flyers. Nor did it have the emotional resonance we were looking for. With commodity status and no money for tangible improvements, we needed to make United's brand voice the differentiator.

We went back to the frequent business travelers. Just as Citi identified with the balance seekers, United had to identify with the aspirations of the FBTs. But unlike Citi, whose target audience was 46 percent of all bank customers, United needed to reach just 9 percent of its customers. This was a smaller, more sophisticated market segment—world citizens who flew a hundred thousand or more miles a year. We needed a more refined insight for this more narrowly defined segment.

Since 1996, we had learned a thing or two about FBTs beyond the fact that they represented 48 percent of revenues. They worked tremendously hard. Success and the trappings of success were very important to them. And FBTs weren't driven only by price. They were brand conscious and more so than most.

When target audience members are brand conscious, they actively seek a brand that reflects their values. The FBTs were hungry for someone to appreciate their efforts, to see them as modern-day heroes, champions of capitalism. United's branding had to articulate how the company was an essential part of the lives of people on the road to success, and that the company clearly understood the energy, drive, and sacrifice it took to succeed.

Identifying the FBTs profile was easy, but identifying *with* them would take finesse. One of the best ways to discover something absolutely fresh is to inventory a category's clichés. We started by looking at the work done in the category—shiny planes taxiing down runways or sailing through the clouds, smiling flight attendants better looking than any you've seen in two decades, easy transit from parking lot to concourse to gate, the beatific smiles of passengers leaning back in their uncharacteristically plush seats—and threw it all out.

Then a bit of magic: there were two senior people on the creative team—an art director from Green Bay, Wisconsin, who had always been a fan of animation, and a copywriter from Bombay, India, who was an accomplished musician. Together they imagined how animation could work with Gershwin's *Rhapsody in Blue,* an enduring part of United Airlines' iconography thanks to our predecessors at Burnett. They came up with a campaign themed "It's Time to Fly" and called for animated commercials—not by just anyone, but by the most talented animation artists in the world.

If you've ever seen any animated shorts at film festivals, you know that there are people out there who have reached unfathomable levels of craft. They are artists with rich imaginations and a compulsive need for perfection. The idea was that the animators would take our vignettes about business travel to a whole new level, dramatically separating United's voice from its competitors. We were betting that the sheer artistry of the work would resonate with the FBTs.

We also didn't want to limit our audience to business travelers. It was important for the FBTs' families and friends to see these spots and share these feelings. This communication needed to be a tribute to the frequent business traveler and had to be seen by everyone in their orbit.

At a preliminary session before the final presentation to John Tague, the animated campaign was declared the runt of the litter, and someone suggested that we leave it at home. We had run into this problem before. Once, after we had made repeated attempts to get an ad approved by U.S. West vice president of marketing John Felt, he told us that he never wanted to see that concept again. We framed it and sent it to him with a request that he hang it on his office wall and observe the comments of people who noticed it. Two weeks later he called and said, "You win—produce it." The ad ran for two years, and was reprinted as a poster for business customers.

With United, we promised to do more work, scrub the bathroom floor, and even pretend to be Chicago Bears fans—with the caveat that "It's Time to Fly" had to be one of the six campaign options presented to Tague. Our self-flagellation paid off. United executives warmed to the animated approach. Tague saw the potential of the ads to connect emotionally, and he appreciated the fact that what he was seeing was radically different from anything else in the category, or any other category for that matter. He also liked the invitational nature of "It's Time to Fly." Most importantly, it fit with the insight about the FBTs. Tague said that the idea was rooted in the insights developed from United's dialogues with its most loyal customers.

Tague was one of those clients who believed in doing the heavy lifting of marketing research before the execution. Many clients test advertising after it's produced. We think it's better to invest in communications strategy, ask the hard questions of the research before the advertising is produced, and then swing for the fences in execution.

"It doesn't feel risky," he said. "It just feels right."[7]

It's Time to Fly

We put out a call to animators from around the world who had been recent nominees for Academy Awards. We were looking for world-class animators who were also extraordinary storytellers.

We chose four animators: one from Russia, one from England, another from Holland, and a team from Canada. Their styles and methods contrasted nicely. By this time, the Fallon creative team had developed the narratives for the commercials. They sent the narratives in written form only—no visuals—and asked the candidates which story they would be most interested in bringing to life in their own style.

Often when we do something different we find ourselves working with partners who represent different skills—specialists we have not worked with before. That calls for an open-minded form of collaboration. We can be control freaks, but we learned a lesson from this campaign: when you bring in talented partners from outside your industry, the art of collaboration requires that you give up control. Gifted people will take you to a higher level if you don't micromanage them.

In a vignette called "Interview," we see a young man as he gets ready for a job interview in a faraway city. The story is simple: a businessperson who thinks he blows his big chance because his shoes don't match. There is no dialogue, only simple, almost photographic images and the Gershwin score, but the execution captures the everyday poignancy of the victories and defeats of business life.

In another, flight attendants smile as they notice a business traveler carefully protecting a long-stemmed rose in his briefcase. As he goes through his busy day of meetings, we can't help wondering what the rose is all about. It turns out that his mother lives in the city he is visiting, and at the end of his busy day, his taxi stops at her house for a visit. The spot launched on Mother's Day.

Right away we saw that animation could tell a story and evoke emotions in a way that simply wouldn't work with actors. The vignettes could have come off as sappy, but the Gersh-

A single frame from "Rose" TV spot. There's majesty in the animation that tran-
scends the story of a man taking time from a business trip to visit his mother. Every
hand-painted cell is a work of art.

win (special arrangements of *Rhapsody in Blue* by members of
the San Francisco Philharmonic) and the artistry of the anima-
tor's work gave us permission to be more overtly emotional.

When we first presented the campaign, our clients could
sense its potential. They then challenged us to prove that "It's
Time to Fly" could be spread more widely throughout the organization. The team set out to integrate these themes and feelings
at every possible contact point with customers. We posted huge
banners at the O'Hare airport and on the sides of buildings in
downtown Chicago. The illustrated art from the print campaign
drove United's direct mail campaign. The flight attendants said,
"It's time to fly" during their in-flight announcements. The in-
flight video also included a mini documentary about each of the
animators. In the months following launch, Fallon worked with

"It's Time to Fly" outdoor ad.   To match the sophistication of the animated campaign, the team used original *The New Yorker* cover art for print and outdoor ads.

United's key communications partners on adapting the campaign's look and feel into hundreds of communications pieces.

On February 29, 2004, the "It's Time to Fly" campaign broke in the perfect venue—the Academy Awards. The reaction was immediately positive. In an advertising category that was almost invisible, people were reacting, writing e-mails and letters to United complimenting the commercials—all proof that we had hit an emotional chord. (We quickly bound 87 of these love notes into a book for the United employees so that they could feel the love—and, we hoped, get a bump in morale.)

Brilliant execution without brilliant strategy is irrelevant, but brilliant strategy without brilliant execution is invisible. If you get both parts of this equation right, you have a chance to improve the return on the investment of your marketing dollars.

Finding the Balance Between Global Consistency and Local Empathy

Beyond the United States, United Airlines walks a strategic tightrope between being a global brand and needing to have people in different business cultures feel like it's an airline that understands them. For United, this means two things: a common look and feel for the brand, and an absolute commitment to connect with local customers (frequent business travelers) on their terms.

In the United States—with its uniquely gung-ho work style—United can say, "Business is a battle. We make the chariots." In contrast, in Europe, which prides itself on more of a balance between work and life and is actively work-shy in places, the tone is more sympathetic and cajoling toward the reluctant business traveler.

Here's where we stand on the emerging trend toward creating advertising that can run in several markets around the world: it's a bad idea. International CFOs look at the cost of TV production in every country and demand one ad that will work around the world. Good luck. By definition, it has to be effective without leveraging the culture of its audience. So no matter how much you can reduce the production budget by producing one culturally challenged commercial, you've given your message almost no chance to extend your media investment by finding its way into local media, the Internet, or the daily life of your prospect.

How can you do your 'Please award us the contract' look if you're on speakerphone?

Opportunities don't come to you, you have to go out and get them. With 12 daily flights and quick and easy connections to 150 US cities, we're the airline to get you there. Book on 0845 844 4777 or at www.unitedairlines.co.uk

It's time to fly℠ **UNITED**
A STAR ALLIANCE MEMBER

United Airlines' European print campaign. When we brought "It's Time to Fly" to Europe, we tweaked the emotional tone of the campaign to align with European attitudes about business and life.

Global strategies should be executed locally. Don't be swayed by famous exceptions to this rule. They are still exceptions. Many were serendipitous; the original execution was local, but so classically human it traveled well.

Because the airline business is operationally driven, the impact of this campaign is hard to separate from United's other initiatives to win back business. For example, the sales force mounted an effective campaign to win commercial contracts. United also found success with other discount and promotional programs on major routes. But even with this caveat, we have compelling evidence that we affected market behavior.

Unaided advertising awareness—where, without prompting, respondents can describe a brand's advertising—is one of the first available metrics for a new campaign. In the first month after "It's Time to Fly" launched, top-of-mind awareness went from 9 percent to 25 percent, the highest of any airline at the time.[8]

Of course, advertising awareness has its limitations as a measure of marketing success. If you don't move the needle, it means you've missed. But if you do move the needle, it simply means that consumers have let you past the first line of defense. You are still a ways from bona fide creative leverage.

We prefer to use preference gains as a measure. In this instance, they were significant. Among *all* business travelers with access to United flights, its rating as "airline most preferred" shot up from 9 percent to 20 percent.[9] Despite financial troubles and an overall soft travel industry, United now had a leading indicator of future sales.

But was it filling seats? In the airline business, there are two crucial business measures. First, there's the system load factor, the ratio of paid seats to available seats. The second critical metric is revenue per available seat mile (RASM). Taken together, system load factor tells you the percentage of paying customers and RASM tells you whether they are paying higher fares or discounted fares.[10] The distance flown is the other variable in this formula, but because routes and schedules were fairly constant, higher yields meant more business travelers.

In March 2004, load factors rose 9.4 percent and continued to rise in the following months. Yields increased in the first and second quarters while declining for the major competitors. All evidence pointed in the right direction; we were winning back share of FBTs.[11] As of this writing, United is poised to exit bankruptcy in the spring of 2006. We hope we played a part.

Art Works

As a legacy airline, United needed to focus on operations. Fighting off bankruptcy was an all-consuming task, and it would have been easy to resist attempts to be creative in marketing and instead find salvation in cost-cutting, organizational streamlining, and other operational gymnastics. Indeed, we often find ourselves stymied because the urgent business of our clients seems to point away from using creativity as a means for positively affecting the bottom line. Not so at United. They never lost sight of the fact that no matter how tough things got, they needed to stay engaged with their customers in a way that transcended the price of a ticket to L.A. We found a way to spark that engagement by first discovering an emotional truth, then using a visual art form to bring that emotion to life. Even in a crisis United found a way to reach out to their best customers, and the effort was rewarded.

Chapter Four

Establishing
and Leveraging
a Category
Advantage

I may not be an actuary, but I did stay
at a Holiday Inn Express last night.

—*Presidential candidate Al Gore, October 2000*

Tonight in the United States, two and a half million travelers will check in to a hotel. Under pressure to keep costs down, a growing number of them will check into a limited-service hotel, made famous by segment leaders Courtyard by Marriott and Hampton Inn. Having exploded in popularity in the 1990s, these "free breakfast bar" hotels offer a clean room and a reasonable chance at a good night's sleep for about $80 per night, with none of the extras that budget-minded travelers don't use.

In 1997, Holiday Inn decided to enter the limited-service hotel fray. The company set up separate goals, marketing teams, and budgets to launch its new chain. (We were already its agency. At first Holiday Inn wanted to hire a separate agency for the new offering, but we persuaded the decision makers that they'd be better off consolidating at one agency that already knew the territory.) The name of the new chain was going to be entirely separate from the Holiday Inn brand. These hotels would be aimed at the budget-minded traveler, but the new brand was going to have a bit of panache. There would be fresh apples at the front desk and free bottled water in the rooms, projecting an overall brand position of health and wellness. You would be "rejuvenated" by staying at there.

These were new properties, and the idea of rejuvenation could be made both physically and conceptually different from the image of Holiday Inn hotels, which were generally older and appealed to a broader, family demographic. Our team was busy creating advertising concepts around the rejuvenation theme, when suddenly we got the call to stop. The franchisees investing in the limited-service concept weren't willing to give up the association with the Holiday Inn name. The entire concept was dead.

Welcome to Holiday Inn Express. The name, a mandate from the top, was both a blessing and a curse. Subbrands and line extensions are a tricky business. A line extension can give the fledgling subsidiary some valuable name recognition and credibility in the category, but often at the expense of its own brand clarity. With Holiday Inn Express, we had to do two things: carve out a place for the brand in a well-established category, and make sure that consumers were clear that this offering was very different from the original brand. Complicating matters was the fact that Holiday Inn was late to the limited-service hotel party: segment leaders Courtyard by Marriott and the Hampton Inn chain had opened in 1983 and 1984, respectively. We had a smaller budget than others in the category did—in fact less than half that of our fiercest competitor. We had no choice but to outsmart rather than outspend.

No "Soft Travelers" Allowed

The target market started out pretty broad: almost everyone stays at these limited-service midpriced hotels. But this wasn't a repeat of the Citibank situation. For one thing, we weren't working with the umbrella brand but with a subbrand. This required that the work be more tactical. We also had to make sure that the new brand didn't encroach on the main brand and cannibalize its sales. Our target audience had to be truly separate in every way.

We've learned over the years that the market segment that matters most is not always the dominant segment in terms of revenues, as it was for United Airlines. Nor does the segment that matters most have to be largest in terms of sheer volume. (As you'll see in the case of Lee Jeans, the critical segment can be the influencers: a small fraction of the audience whose brand behavior drives the rest of the market.)

In the case of Holiday Inn Express, we homed in on the real road warriors: independent businesspeople who usually travel on their own dime or on a small per diem and not a big expense account. They weren't likely to cannibalize Holiday Inn's base of leisure travelers, and they would make ideal regular customers. These were customers who could easily rack up one hundred hotel stays a year, the kind of guys (and most of them were men) who went to Cedar Rapids on Monday, drove to Des Moines on Tuesday, and then made a final call in Sioux Falls on Thursday before heading back home to Davenport.

The next step was to listen to these people and learn how they thought and felt about the category. Was there fertile ground the competition hadn't yet claimed? We put together ten focus groups in three parts of the country and invited road warriors only. As with Citi, the idea was simply to explore, to watch for the energy of these people and test our insight that they were a good target market.

As it turned out, these people were fun, interesting, and sociable, and they loved to tell travel stories. They weren't entirely dissatisfied with the competition's offerings, but they didn't feel that any brands were courting them. This was when we knew we were sniffing around a potentially big idea. When an influential segment feels it isn't being paid attention to, you have an opportunity for effective marketing communication.

Now seemed a good time to do some ethnographic research. As we have said before, a focus group can be a useful tool in the right circumstances, but ideally you have to get out of the office, live with a target market and observe them up close and personal. To gain a deeper understanding of the lives of business road warriors, we needed to see the world through their windshields.

So we hit the road with them. Our planners videotaped the road warriors while they drove cross-country. We talked to them about their work, their families, and their daily experiences. One account planner barreled down Highway 70 with a guy who was like John Candy's character in the movie *Planes, Trains, and Automobiles.* This character saw business as one and the same with the romance and hard work of the road. He said that reservations were for "soft travelers."

The world of concierges and fluffy, unused bathrobes were anathema to this tribe of travelers. We no longer called them road warriors. We called them "drive-ups," after their habit of working and traveling for ungodly hours and then driving up to their night's lodgings at the very last minute. They were salt-of-the-earth business easy riders with a lot of territory to cover. Many were entrepreneur owners of start-ups who were watching their costs. Ultimately what they wanted was control of their environment—to travel on their terms. They wanted the basics, not luxuries they would never use. After all, who needed a concierge with a British accent on Thursday night in Sioux Falls?

As with United, a psychological profile started to emerge, and, like United's frequent business travelers, the drive-ups wanted respect. The emotional color of this desire differed, however, because the drive-ups were a middle-class demographic. They wouldn't have responded to the grandeur of "It's Time to Fly." They had dreams and aspirations, but doing the work itself was the emotional reward. They were working hard and working smart, and that was going to be their ticket to success.

Our research showed us that the drive-ups got more than a good night's rest when they stayed at a limited-service hotel; they got an emotional reward, too. These experienced business travelers had wisely opted for only the necessities, and not the superfluous extras, and they felt savvy for having made a practical choice. Interestingly, they told us that this feeling stayed with them well beyond the transaction, and this told us that making a smart choice had a higher emotional value than the more mundane pleasure of simply getting a good deal.

The team began to consider how applauding the drive-ups' pragmatic wisdom could reinforce the rational value proposition of the limited-service category. A message about smartness, delivered in a refreshing or countercategory way, might allow us to strategically establish Holiday Inn Express within the segment. In other words, we could make inexpensive more than just a bargain—we could make it cool.

Ironically, there was nothing proprietary about this. If Marriott or Hampton had claimed the same territory, there was nothing we could have done about it. But they hadn't. A quick study of advertising in the category revealed that the competition was focused almost exclusively on amenities. Their ads featured pictures of well-landscaped properties, and the copy promised a free newspaper of your choice and a breakfast buffet better than the other guy's. If we could create a "smart" persona that distinguished the brand from competitors (and from Holiday Inn), then we could own the emotion for the entire category.

No, but I Did Stay at a Holiday Inn Express Last Night

At a couple of very tough meetings in Atlanta, we failed to come up with anything substantial around this theme. We had the overall idea but were having trouble simplifying the execution, and the client's patience was running out. Then late one night the veteran copywriter who had been wrestling with this problem was standing at the corner of 11th and Hennepin in downtown Minneapolis when "Stay Smart" popped into his head. The best themes seem so natural that it's hard to imagine they weren't the first idea on the legal pad.

We went down to Atlanta with several campaigns built around "Stay Smart." In our favorite, the campaign featured a person who stepped up in some kind of emergency and brilliantly saved the day, and then announced that he was no expert but had stayed in a Holiday Inn Express the night before.

In the first spot, for example, a group of tourists in a national park stare helplessly as a woman is confronted by a grizzly bear. Our hero appears from nowhere and takes control, shouting instructions to the woman that help her defuse the situation and escape. "Are you a park ranger?" someone asks. The response in every single spot is exactly the same: "No, but I did stay at a Holiday Inn Express last night."

The spot was unexpected and damn funny. We knew from our face-to-face meetings that these road warriors would positively identify with our fearless, common sense hero. Holiday Inn Express President John Sweetwood and Marketing Director Tom Seddon also liked this approach. They could see how the target audience would respond to the brand, and they liked how we had brought an absurd sense of humor to a category that was usually handled with a straight face. The executives gave us the thumbs-up in spite of the obvious shortcoming from a franchisee's perspective: the spots never showed the property, the rooms, nor the smiling, helpful staff.

With a small national media budget and the fact that we had recommended TV as the primary medium, our clients had to make one more leap of faith. We promised that if they

Video: Bear roaring

Man: That's *Urus Octos,* ma'am. Grizzly bear. About 1200 pounds. Try and act confident. Show your teeth and snarl. It should trigger his flight instinct. If that doesn't work, walk directly up to the bear and box him on his ears.

Woman: Are you a forest ranger?

Man: No, but I did stay at a Holiday Inn Express last night.

Super: It won't make you smarter. But you will feel smarter.

Holiday Inn Express, "Bear," 1998.
We've created more than twenty TV spots for Holiday Inn Express, and even we've been surprised at the legs of this campaign, which has been running for more than seven years. You can see this spot at www.juicingtheorange.com. Click on "See the Work."

would let us make provocative and fun TV spots for Holiday Inn Express, they in turn would get an additional return on their advertising investment from watercooler buzz and press mentions. We hoped we could make the "Stay Smart" campaign a phenomenon that jumped the tracks of paid media and became a nugget of popular culture.

Very little advertising ever finds its way into the popular culture, but when it does, we've seen our clients enjoy high returns on their investment. In the late 1980s, for example, we convinced Timex that its abandoned slogan "It takes a licking and keeps on ticking" had value beyond the promise of durability. For the television campaign, we brought back the torture tests, but as a parody of the old spots; our tongue was firmly planted in our cheek. A Timex strapped to the stomach of a Sumo wrestler survives the bout. An operatic soprano hits a high note that shatters glass but not the faceplate on her Timex. Ad awareness jumped 30 percent, but more important, the campaign generated free publicity as the ads were talked about on *Entertainment Tonight*, the *Oprah Winfrey Show*, and *Late Night with David Letterman*, and were even mentioned in *Time* magazine. The calculated value was more than half a million dollars.

This symbiotic relationship between marketing communications and pop culture is mysterious, but exploiting that relationship is sometimes the key to creative leverage. Our goal as an organization is to understand culture so well that we can use its idioms and nuances to transcend blatant selling messages. We don't always see the signs that something will click. Remember the wonderful gravelly voiced old woman whose "Where's the beef?" line for Wendy's became part of pop culture, political speeches, and bad jokes in the late 1980s? That wasn't our ad. In fact, we had used the same actress, Clara Peller, for a commercial about a year earlier, but we overdubbed her voice because we thought she sounded too weird.

But we thought that the campaign for Holiday Inn Express might be one of those times when we could connect with pop culture. Why? What were the clues? The first clue was in-house. Our creative teams are not protective of their work; they show it to other creative teams for feedback. The threshold for an approving nod is high, but if the place is abuzz then we know we could be on to something. The second acid test comes when the storyboards go out to directors for bid. If A-list directors are willing to change their schedules and lower their day rates, that's another very good sign.

But the most telling clue in this case was the drive-ups themselves. They were the kind of gregarious guys who repeat lines from *Saturday Night Live* or a Chris Rock HBO special. One-liners were a part of their social currency. "No, but I did stay at a Holiday Inn Express last night" was exactly the kind of catchphrase they could adopt as their own.

The next question was how to plant the seed.

Television Ads for People Who Are Never Home

The Holiday Inn Express national TV budget was so small that the media buy had to be surgically precise. We learned from our ethnographic research that the drive-ups usually made their plans on Sundays or Mondays. This was also supported in Holiday Inn's operational reports; these were the days of lowest hotel occupancy.

We placed Holiday Inn Express advertising only on Sundays and Mondays, when we thought we might catch our target audience at home. We also placed the spots on the few cable stations they told us they relied on: ESPN, CNN, and the Weather Channel. This meant that we had a shot at owning their TV environment and looking like big players. (We always choose to have a larger presence in a few places rather than a smaller presence in more places. When we started what is now Fallon Worldwide, we ran one full-page ad in the Minneapolis *Star-Tribune* rather than run quarter-pages four times. We looked a lot bigger and more important than five people hanging out their shingle with no clients.)

As we had hoped, the campaign caught on almost immediately and became a much-referenced pop culture phenomenon. "No, but I did stay at a Holiday Inn Express last night" was quickly picked up by the on-air personalities at ESPN, where we were running a heavy schedule. But soon the *Chicago Tribune*, the *Washington Post*, David Letterman, NPR, and editorial cartoons saw fit to use our line. And like "Where's the beef?" it even made the presidential campaign stump (this time courtesy of Al Gore).

Typically, paid media is measured in impressions: the number of people who see the message multiplied by the number of exposures. The unpaid references that appeared in the content part of programs or newspapers added more than one hundred million impressions. We consider popular media coverage, if it's positive and on message, to be a strong indicator that we are generating a lot of talk value. We quickly found that if we Googled "No, but I did stay at a Holiday Inn Express last night" we got hundreds of mentions. In the hotel

Video: Open on a research laboratory. It is extremely white and very sterile looking. We see a number of scientists in laboratory suits. One scientist is lecturing the others. His voice has the amplified sound that is necessary to speak through these suits. He is looking into a microscope.

Scientist 1: This is a very rare strain of the A5 virus—it produces mRNA, the deadliest of the stem-loop structures.

Video: As he says this, he looks into the microscope and accidentally knocks over a vial that has the virus in it. It shatters on the floor. Cut to a close-up of the other scientists— they have absolutely horrified looks on their faces. Cut to a close-up of the lecturer. He is very calm.

Scientist 1: Oh, don't worry. It's not an airborne strain.

Scientist 2: Excuse me, how long have you been studying the A5 virus?

Scientist 1: Well, I'm not actually a scientist (he frames the word "scientist" with his gloved hands as he speaks), but I did stay at a Holiday Inn Express last night.

Video: One of the scientists faints.

Cut to final frames and logo.

Super: Stay smart. Stay at a Holiday Inn Express.

category, Holiday Inn Express's brand theme was the only one that had any presence. Our brand was getting noticed by the target audience, and the best part was that our client didn't have to pay for all the exposure.

As the campaign evolved, we began to use the line to celebrate individuals who not only were smart but also had performed in situations that were way over their heads. In a 2001 favorite, Holiday Inn Express guests perform incognito as the rock band KISS the day after their stay. In a 2002 spot, *Jeopardy*'s Alex Trebek is increasingly annoyed by a dorky guy who keeps on winning. The contestant finally admits that he stayed at a Holiday Inn Express last night.

PR professionals don't like to refer to nonadvertising publicity as *unpaid* media. They prefer the term *earned* media. We concur. That's the whole point about creative leverage. It earns its way into the popular culture, well beyond the paid media investment. To calculate the dollar value of popular media coverage, think of it as getting exposure within a program, like product placement. A mention on ESPN's *SportsCenter*, for example, would be given the value of a thirty-second spot on that same program. By that reckoning, Holiday Inn Express got more than a million dollars' worth of additional coverage.

There's no question that the "Stay Smart" campaign delivered. This latecomer subbrand is now leading the pack. Holiday Inn Express ad awareness is more than double that of any

Opposite: Holiday Inn Express, "A5 Virus, 2000." This creative concept was extremely flexible; all we needed was a dramatic emergency where our hero comes to the rescue with a brilliant solution. Every new ad seemed to drive the catchphrase further into popular culture. You can see this spot at www.juicingtheorange.com. Click on "See the Work."

other chain in the category. Brand awareness is up twenty-seven points, and competitors remain flat.[1] More important than raw awareness, a look at brand imagery explains the business advantage the "Stay Smart" campaign delivered. What's interesting about these image factors is that "good value for the money" shows the smallest advantage. Its brand momentum allows Holiday Inn Express to be at the upper end of category pricing.

The net result was bottom-line business results for Holiday Inn Express. The industry metric is revenues per available room (RevPAR). Holiday Inn Express is growing at 15 percent, compared with 9 percent for the category. (Starting with only 850 properties when the advertising broke in 1999, there are now 1,350 Holiday Inn Expresses across the United States.)[2] Today Holiday Inn Express is the hands-down segment growth leader; the chain is years ahead of plan.

In 2004, *Brandweek* featured Jenifer Zeigler, senior vice president of global brand management for InterContinental Hotels and Resorts, as one of its "Marketers of the Next Generation" for her bold leadership of the brand.[3] Zeigler is quick to give the "Stay Smart" campaign its fair share of credit for the business success. "We have a rock solid operational model, and our franchisees are doing a great job of consistently delivering on the brand promise," she says. "But make no mistake about it. The level of familiarity and momentum we enjoy is due to the Stay Smart campaign. It's an advantage our competitors would love to have, and Fallon has done a great job of finding fresh ways to keep it working, even when we have to get tactical."[4]

The "Smart" insight informed the entire the Holiday Inn Express business strategy. Even today, this small but signifi-

The advantage of staying smart

By 2003, Holiday Inn Express was clearly the leader in image considerations that drive business and had the brand momentum necessary to keep it going.

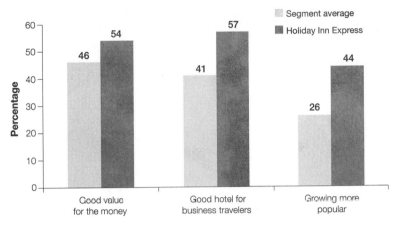

Source: Millward Brown, 2003.

cant emotional connection focuses the franchises and their staff. The "Stay Smart" platform is integrated at every point of customer contact: in-hotel marketing posters, in-room post-cards and sales tools, services, and systems. The Holiday Inn Express coffee is branded Smart Roast. We've even found ways to extend the joke with guests. If the reservation line is busy, you hear classical music, accompanied by a reminder that classical music is good for your brain.

A young brand, Holiday Inn Express has quickly developed a reputation as the limited-service category leader. Distinctions include "Top hotel choice for entrepreneurs" by *Entrepreneur*, "Top hotel brand in its segment" by *Business Travel News*, and the Travel Industry Association's 2001

Odyssey Award for Travel Advertising. The New York American Marketing Association EFFIE awards have consistently recognized "Stay Smart" as one of America's most effective advertising campaigns. The brand has been honored with a total of five EFFIEs, including the most recent in 2004: a Gold award in the Sustained Success category, in which entrants must prove business results for at least five years.

Still Smart

One of the goals of marketing communications is to make the consumer, and by extension the culture, your ally. What else besides creativity can do this for you? Increased media spending can make your voice louder in the marketplace, but can't force people to listen. Only a campaign that makes a genuine human connection with the audience can invite the consumer to participate in your message.

In the fall of 2005, six years after the brand was launched, we are still getting free mentions in the media. An editorial cartoon in a major daily featured controversial Supreme Court candidate Harriet Miers responding to challenges about her qualifications with the line, "I've never been a judge, but I did stay at a Holiday Inn Express last night." That night, CNN newscaster Jeanne Moos repeated the caption on the air. Creative leverage has a life of its own.

Chapter Five

Overcoming a Serious Branding Problem

C ompared with the U.S. automotive market, where seventeen million vehicles are sold each year, the British auto market is smaller but no less intense. Even though only two and a half million vehicles are sold each year, the British rival the Americans in terms of their love of the automobile. Great Britain has more and better automotive magazines than the United States, and they have a wider following. The British have always had a special car culture of their own, with legendary race drivers like Nigel Mansell, Sir Stirling Moss, and Sir Jack Brabham as well as legendary motorcars like Rolls-Royce, MG, Jaguar, and Bentley.

In 1999, our client, automotive manufacturer Skoda UK, had less than 1 percent market share. In its size category, it competed with other small imports such as Lada, Citroën, Seat, and Fiat, as well as stalwarts like Ford, VW, and Mazda. Because of the dominance of the bigger players, the smaller manufacturers

The perception of Skoda. Here's what came to mind when England thought of Skoda in the 1980s and 1990s.

like Skoda were locked into the discount niche, but this wasn't the brand's problem. Many companies have thrived by offering a bargain. Skoda was facing stagnant growth thanks to a brand identity that was crushing its best efforts.

If you spent time in Europe in the 1980s, the only Skodas you saw were driven by communists vacationing in the West. The cars were small—even by compact standards—and had a flimsy quality that made them seem like tin toys. They were also slow and prone to break down. You couldn't buy one in the rest of Western Europe before the Iron Curtain came down, but an importer had been selling the ugly little cars in Great Britain for twenty years.

The Skoda had a special place in British culture. The car's looks and mechanical shortcomings supplied British humorists with endless material. If the Communist-era Skoda product itself was suspect, the brand's image was off-the-scale bad. In England there were Web sites devoted to Skoda jokes.[1] The British tabloid press never missed an opportunity to stick it to the ugly little car from the former Czechoslovakia. "I still think it's slightly less embarrassing to be seen getting out of the back of a sheep than getting out of the back of a Skoda," one writer quipped in the *Daily Mirror*.[2]

But after the Iron Curtain fell, Skoda was acquired by Volkswagen, and Skoda's engineering quality rose to VW levels. Skodas were built using better materials, and their service records improved. Unfortunately, British consumers knew nothing about the surge in quality, and even if they had, the brand image was so bad it might not have mattered. Throughout the 1990s, Skoda UK produced high-quality cars to almost universal laughter.

Skoda wasn't entirely hopeless. Although it was mocked as a brand, Skoda's UK sales grew through the mid-1990s, and some of its customers—the independent souls who were savvy enough to see past the image—were extraordinarily loyal. At the same time, Skoda was stuck. Like a lot of brands saddled with major image problems, Skoda wasn't making inroads into the broader consumer market. It served an eccentric niche of budget drivers who took a perverse pleasure in the derision they received, but 60 percent of people surveyed said they'd still reject a Skoda out of hand.[3] The company learned how dire the situation was when it launched the new Octavia in 1998. Thanks to the product transformation led by Volkswagen, the Octavia was by all accounts a fine car. The reviews were flattering, and the car's $17.9 million launch advertising budget was Skoda's largest ever. Skoda braced itself for success.

The launch was a disaster. In 1998, Skoda sold only 2,569 Octavias. Skoda's brand image was unaffected, with no significant image improvements recorded over the launch period. The advertising costs were a stunning $7,000 per car.

The failure, in retrospect, was one of strategy. The Octavia's marketing had been model-specific and product-centered, targeted at Skoda's small but loyal following. In short, Skoda was behaving like a brand without a problem.

In 1999, Skoda conceded that it needed a new approach if its next launch—the Fabia supermini—was to succeed. Skoda's director of marketing, Chris Hawken, had come from Volkswagen. Based on a previous relationship with Fallon London's founding partners, we were invited to pitch for the Fabia supermini.

Given what we knew about the failed launch of the Octavia, we knew we needed to dig deep. You can divide the problem-solving work of creativity into a diagnosis phase and an execution phase. If you get the diagnosis wrong, the creativity you apply to the execution will be, at best, entertaining, and the business problem will remain unsolved. (We'd been there before. Our first campaign for United was artful and elegant in its claim that United was "rising." But air travelers didn't see it that way. Because Skoda was starting from a disadvantaged position, we couldn't afford to have the same credibility problem.) As we had with Purina, our initial diagnosis was that consumers needed to be educated. If people only knew how great Skodas had become, they wouldn't laugh at them anymore.

But because we hadn't worked with this brand before, we underestimated the extent of Skoda's problem. Hawken knew better. As a passionate advocated for Skoda, Hawken was enraged by the injustice of his brand's stigma. The Octavia had been a fine new model, brilliantly engineered by Volkswagen, praised by the motor press, but the car never got a fair shake. "It was so out of hand," said Hawken, "dealers reported that children would quietly sob in the showroom when they imagined their parents dropping them off at school in a Skoda."

Even after hearing these anecdotes, we didn't quite grasp the enormity of what Hawken was telling us. We went back to the shop thinking that we could bludgeon the market into submission, citing the Fabia supermini's brilliant engineering, as vouched for by a highly credible automotive press (whose serious praise of the new Skoda was nearly universal). But when the account people and planners shared this brief with the creative team, the copywriters and art directors said, "Yes, but it's still a Skoda."

Now we got it. Our London creative team's instinctive reaction to our business-as-usual plan made us recall author Randall Rothenberg's observation that automobiles are mechanical sports jackets.[4] Most people won't get in a car unless the brand feels right for them. The creative team's instincts told us that in order to win this account we had to ignore everything we knew about traditional automotive advertising and come at Skoda's brand problem more essentially. In this sobering moment, we realized we had to start from scratch.

Owning the Joke

Skoda UK's brand problem was a thorny one. Humor is a wonderful communications tool when you're the one making people laugh. Being on the business end of a joke is another thing altogether. Anyone who was ever made fun of in junior high knows that it's almost impossible to fight back when you're the subject of ridicule. At least in a social setting you have the chance to face your tormentors. But what can a brand do?

We always try to remind ourselves that a brand lives almost entirely in the minds of consumers, and there's no guarantee that they will be fair or reasonable or well informed. You can change people's minds, but only if they first give you permission, and that won't happen if they think you're a joke.

You must first meet them where they are. In this case, the emotional truth of the brand was not difficult to ferret out, as it was with Citi and Holiday Inn Express. Skoda's emotional truth didn't need discovery. It was unavoidable. The more we tried to work around the stigma, the more we realized that we would have to face the Skoda joke head-on. The job at hand wasn't to introduce a car, but to change the social currency of the brand. As one of our partners in Fallon's London office said, "We needed to manage the ether."

When we finally accepted this idea, we were in a position to make some progress. We were not only going to acknowledge the stigma, but also embrace it like a long-lost relative. We were going to own it, because you can't make fun of someone who is already doing a better job of making fun of themselves.

It was time to define the business problem as clearly as possible. We wrote down this simple thought: "Skoda Fabia is better than you think."

There are data moments when you discover something about your customer that changes everything, and there are big idea moments when you know instantly that you have discovered the simple thought that will begin your journey out of the wilderness. Shoulder muscles relax. Smiles appear. This understated sentence helped us acknowledge the elephant in the room and move past it.

The next step was to turn that idea into ads. The team brainstormed taglines; the one that made the final cut was, "It's a Skoda. Honest." This was perfect. Four words that we could run next to the Fabia supermini—which really is a smart-looking car—and trumpet the beauty of this new automobile while acknowledging the stigma.

The next step, in parallel with creating the television ads, was to propose a media plan. Again, we returned to the key insight and realized that our media buys would have to be broad. We needed to court the press (press coverage was part of the problem, and so it had to be part of the solution) and reach everyone who had ever laughed at a Skoda joke. This campaign had to be the opposite of the precise targeting we did to reach Holiday Inn Express's drive-ups. Instead of narrowcasting or trying to use market research to pinpoint the ideal Skoda customer, we would tell the world.

Up to this point, we were still competing with two other agencies for the account. Now we had to share our provocative recommendations and we were nervous. Every small agency covets a car account. The team knew that they had nailed it, but did we have the courage to tell our prospective client that our brilliant solution required that they publicly admit their cars were a joke?

When it came time to present to Skoda, we didn't softpedal the risk. We warned the Skoda marketers: swallow your pride; you're not going to like what we're going to say. We then explained why it was critical to attack the stigma head-on or else risk the "brilliant engineering" message falling on deaf ears. Even for those who were prepared to consider buying a Skoda, the biggest barrier was an irrational prejudice against the brand. The role of advertising therefore was to confront that prejudice. The target audience for advertising had to be the British public at large. The aim was to make potential buyers confident that they could choose a Skoda without being laughed at.

Then it was time to show the Skoda marketing team the work we had devised. The first spot opened with a group of people touring a modern automotive factory, where the beautiful new cars are rolling down the assembly line. Suddenly a guy who hasn't been paying much attention says, "And I hear you also make those funny little Skoda cars here as well."

In the second concept, a weary young executive enters an underground parking ramp late in the evening after all the other cars are gone. The security guard rushes up to him to report that something terrible has happened to his new car. As they approach the car, the guard apologizes profusely for not catching the vandal who put a Skoda emblem on the shiny new sedan.

Both concepts featured people who still thought Skoda cars were crap, and by gently ridiculing this attitude, we encouraged consumers to conclude that they weren't one of those people.

Chris Hawken said, "I get it, but do we have to do this?" We told him yes. We said we'd tried alternatives, but we honestly couldn't find another answer. The managing director, a Skoda veteran with an accounting background, said, "You are

Skoda, "Factory Tour," 2000. This spot gives viewers plenty of time to see the new Fabia from every angle and learn some important facts about it. Then the dolt makes the stupid comment, and the running Skoda joke begins to reverse itself. You can see this spot at www.juicingtheorange.com. Click on "See the Work."

Video: We hear the discussion as a group of executives tours a very modern and efficient automotive assembly plant.

Man 1: This is where the body parts are made, sir.

Man 2: This is absolutely enormous.

Man 1: The car has a 10-year anti-corrosion warranty.

Man 2: Really?

Man 1: We have 240 robots here.

Man 2: Marvelous. Oh, look at that. Incredible.

Man 1: Oh, stand back.

Man 2: Hello.

Man 1: This is the first car in its class to meet the new European emissions standards for the year 2005.

Man 2: I must say, I think this is terribly impressive.

Man 1: Every single car is individually tested before it can leave the factory.

Man 2: Every car?

Man 1: Yes.

Man 1: And this, sir, is the finished article.

Man 2: It's wonderful. Well done. And I hear you also make those funny little Skoda cars here as well.

Super: The new Fabia. It's a Skoda. Honest.

about to ask me to spend millions of pounds on a television campaign that features people saying my car is crap?"

A Strategic Leap of Faith

Skoda put the TV concepts from all three agencies into consumer testing. The research company reported that all three were likable, but the "It's a Skoda. Honest." approach was the clear winner. We were awarded the account.

Before the new model launched, the managing director of Skoda in Prague wanted a briefing. The meeting was scheduled for a Sunday evening at a Heathrow airport hotel. Signals got crossed, and the big boss landed at Gatwick and then endured a long cab ride to Heathrow. With that inauspicious beginning, we presented our work as best we could. "I don't understand it," the chief of Skoda said. "I don't approve it. Proceed if you must. I'm powerless to stop you. It's not right for our brand." And he flew back to Prague.

After much soul-searching, Chris Hawken put his career on the line and persuaded his boss to launch the campaign. Why? He believed owning the joke was the best chance of getting Skoda noticed and considered—something that needed to happen if the company was to achieve a breakthrough. (As a result of his bold decision, Hawken was dropped from Skoda's European marketing council even before the campaign broke.)

The Skoda Fabia supermini campaign launched as planned in February 2000. In order to make as much immediate impact as possible, the team front-loaded the media buy. Unlike Holiday Inn Express, which had the luxury of growing over time, the Skoda campaign needed to provoke an instant press reaction, and ideally one that talked about how the campaign changed the popular joke.

Fortunately, "It's a Skoda. Honest." played out in the press exactly as we had hoped.

> *"History's biggest comeback since Bobby Ewing stepped out of the shower,"* said the Mirror. *"The new VW-owned Skoda is hip and sexy—yes, sexy."*[5]
>
> *"I have a sneaking suspicion that Skodas are about to become extremely fashionable,"* said the Spectator.[6]
>
> The Guardian *reported, "The way things are now, Rolls Royce can only benefit from association with Skoda."*[7] *(At the time, a venerable but distressed national treasure, Rolls-Royce was in the news as a takeover target by both VW and BMW.)*

The year 2000 was a giddy one for Skoda. After only one burst of advertising, key image measures were up. The campaign made a dramatic impact on "consideration." Previously, prospects had ignored Skoda's product innovations and previous marketing efforts, resulting in high rejection numbers. In a company first, the number of prospects who would not consider Skoda dropped from 60 percent to 42 percent, a rejection figure lower than the equivalent figures for Fiat and Citroën. Since that initial burst, the top box measure of "active consideration" has grown from 18 percent to a peak of 28 percent.[8]

Another immediate and lasting effect was on the Skoda dealers. Just as Skoda's dealers had become accustomed to nearly empty showrooms, they had also gotten used to ignoring or even perversely celebrating the brand's negative image. Our

Less funny, more tire kickers

There is nothing to laugh at here. These were encouraging early indicators that we had gotten it right.

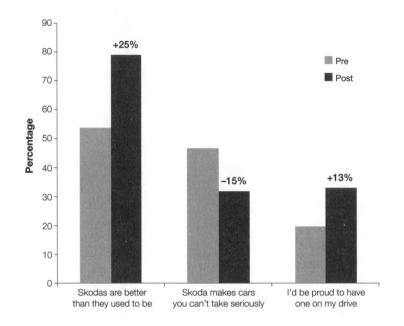

Source: Millward Brown, July 2000.

campaign might have created a wave of opposition from dealers—Why rock the boat? Just tell them it's a cheap Volkswagen!

In 2001, Britain's car dealers rated Skoda "best make" in terms of product advertising by manufacturers because the campaign was high profile and generated so much new showroom traffic or what the British call "footfall."[9] Even better, the advertising had created a heightened sense of expectations that dealers felt they had to match. The advertising push ushered in an upgrade in retail standards. The consumer got a better car, a better brand, and better service; the retailers got more customers and more sales at higher prices and better margins than ever before.

Collectively, the Skoda campaign had a striking business impact. Without increasing the number of Skoda dealers, volume growth easily outstripped the market, winning record 80 percent market share growth for the brand. (Prices actually increased 60 percent between 1997 and 2001, with more modest increases after that. Unlike in the discounted American market, Skoda was by no means buying market share.) Sales jumped from twenty thousand cars annually in 1999 to thirty-three thousand in 2001. The rate of increase in sales in Great Britain was three times the rate of growth for Skoda in the rest of Europe.[10]

The Fabia supermini relaunch was the start of an amazing two-year period for Skoda. "It's a Skoda. Honest." reinvigorated the brand's marketing program, which added a new brand-led direct marketing campaign, point-of-sale materials, and a Web site. For the direct mail campaign, thousands of actual Skoda car emblems were mailed to prospects, with the invitation to simply live with it for a while. During the campaign period, direct mail response rates doubled compared to prior response rates and contributed to more than two thousand sales.[11]

Here's another interesting point: remember the unhappy 1998 launch of the Octavia model we mentioned at the beginning? Skoda wisely relaunched the Octavia. Even though spending was half the original launch investment, the sales effect was double.

You can't put a price on having the last laugh, but we had that, too. The press continued to champion the new Skoda brand image long after the campaign launched. In 2002, the *Sun* said, "The Czech manufacturer has gone from motoring joke to huge success story in just a few short years."[12] An advertising trade magazine analyzed it succinctly: "The brand's existing memorability—a poisoned chalice if ever there was one—is made into a plus. How stupid the mistaken fools in the ad are, thinks the viewer, who ten seconds ago wasn't aware of what the new Fabia looked like either. The commercials tell us something and make us feel superior about knowing it with the speed of light. How clever is that?"[13]

A Hard Risk Worth Taking

In hindsight, the risk Skoda took in owning the joke looks prudent or even obvious. Skoda had just failed on an expensive product launch. It had tested the campaign against strong alternatives. They knew they needed to win over the press.

At the time, however, joining in on the national joke was not easy, but the lesson here is not the moment when the campaign launched. The London office taught us that courage is a process not an event. There were risks at every step in the development of this campaign and many opportunities to back down. The Fallon team could have done something more conventional to win their first car account. Skoda's marketing team could have taken an easier route. The dealers could have rejected the campaign and gone their own way. Instead, everyone involved embraced the risk and reaped the rewards.

A final note: Chris Hawken went on to bigger and better things in the Volkswagen organization as general manager of marketing for Volkswagen SE Asia Pacific (and, once again, became a client of Fallon—this time, our Singapore office). In Adam Morgan's book *The Pirate Inside,* Hawken is featured as one of those brave renegades who change the course of corporate cultures.[14]

Chapter Six

Reviving a Mature Consumer Brand

Lee is for my Mom and her fat-ass friends.

—*Teenager in a focus group, 1997*[1]

n 1987, when we first started working with Lee Jeans, annual sales of denim topped $6 billion, and the youth segment drove the volume in the category.[2] (Today, annual sales are around $14.6 billion.)[3] At the time, Levi's was the undisputed king of the hill. Lee was a classic underdog brand.

During our entire eighteen-year relationship with Lee, we constantly faced marketplace challenges in this highly volatile category. First, there was the era of designer jeans. In the 1980s and early 1990s, designer brands such as Calvin Klein, Guess, and Girbaud captured share from both Lee and Levi's, but Lee was especially hard hit. That trend also changed the retail landscape. Consumers no longer went to department stores such as JC Penney or Sears to buy new jeans, and there were a growing numbers of specialty shops (Old Navy, Gap, Abercrombie & Fitch, The Limited, Urban Outfitters) that either had private-label brands or didn't stock Lee.

Compounding the distribution problems was the brand's image with young people. For nearly two decades, the Lee brand had grown its business nicely by appealing to a certain generation of women (now thirty-five and older) but at the expense of alienating young people. Here at the agency, those of us who had teenage kids could get Lee jeans for free—but our own teenagers found them so uncool, they wouldn't wear them in a public high school.

In 1996, we thought we finally found the sweet spot—a stylish and poignant campaign that would make Lee cool again. We did a series of boy-meets-girl spots shot in black and white that were as well executed as anything we'd done. In one spot, an eighteen-year-old boy bashfully approaches a girl in jeans on a ferryboat. He holds out a locket. "You dropped this," he tells her. "Where?" she asks. "In Nebraska," he says. The campaign tested very well, and the ads ran all over the place—on *Friends*, *Seinfeld*, and all the other top-rated shows. A daughter of one of our employees, a college freshman, reported that the girls in her dorm were repeating the dialogue from the Lee ads.

You might think that we had another Holiday Inn Express on our hands, but this campaign was a great example of how you can execute a perfect spot but fail on a more fundamental level. Sales of Lee Jeans remained resolutely stagnant.

Why? Because we soon discovered we were fixing the surface problem but not addressing Lee's underlying brand problem. Lee didn't have the same kind of problem we saw with Skoda automobiles; the jeans company was not a national joke. But we had nevertheless forgotten to start the conversation where the consumer was.

In the jeans category, that meant addressing the frame of mind of the eighteen-year-olds who drive the purchase patterns of their peer group. Every brand in an eighteen-year-old's mind has an assigned cool factor, and only the most confident and coolest of their group can change the assigned rating. These "influencers" dictate brand behavior for a frighteningly large circle. The reality of the category was this: the trendsetters wore Levi's. Moms wore Lee jeans. Everybody at school knew that.

It became clear that our target market simply couldn't *believe* that these spots could be associated with the Lee brand. To most of them, these hip boy-meets-girl vignettes were instinctively about the Levi's brand, not Lee. While different executionally from Levi's, our advertising was thematically in Levi's territory, not Lee's. Even though the ads tested well, more than 60 percent of consumers who saw them air *assumed* they were Levi's commercials because Lee wasn't sexy—Levi's was. Name misappropriation was a long-term problem for Lee because of the unfortunate similarity of their brand to the more popular Levi's. We compounded that problem by trying to own someone else's emotion.

Our failures aside, by 1997 Lee was at a critical juncture. Its share with young men had hovered in the single digits for a decade. Meanwhile, Levi's had grown to a dominant 50 percent share. Gap, Old Navy, Abercrombie & Fitch, and others were expanding their presence and youth-culture coolness. Lee's problems were intensifying to the point that retailers were losing faith in the brand as a whole. They didn't believe Lee understood the youth market, and they were questioning the long-term viability of the Lee brand.

For Lee to turn its brand around, it would have to take a risk. Tackling the youth-market problem would require a total company commitment and the bulk of its meager marketing dollars, which in turn meant undersupporting its current business base of women. Fortunately, there was a wholesale turnover in the teams that guided the Lee brand, and we assigned an entirely new Fallon team as well. Everyone knew that the situation was desperate—the perfect situation for creative leverage to shine.

Indestructible Spirit

The first thing the agency team did was to conduct a complete business analysis. We do this exercise not only when we're pitching business but also with existing clients when we're stuck. Our planners pored over all the data they could find about jeans, fashion, and retail trends. Then the team called an offsite meeting at the Marriott hotel near Lee headquarters in Overland Park, Kansas, to present the findings.

One noteworthy discovery was that 25 percent of Lee's sales were coming through its own outlet store. This figure had crept up so slowly over time that it had failed to trigger an alarm, but it signaled to our team that there was frighteningly little consumer demand at the retail level. Otherwise, the insights into the category were not surprising, although they did help to refocus the team and the client on the following truths:

1. *The money is in youth.* Young people buy more and spend more on jeans than any other demographic. This seems obvious, but Lee had enjoyed what success it had with twenty-five- to thirty-five-year-old women, and having the facts in front of us helped support taking the risk to try to go younger.

2. *The money is in college-age men.* Our research showed that most people cement their apparel brand affiliations by the age of twenty-four. Naturally, we would have to build our relationships sooner, but not too soon: boys in their early teens are too busy experimenting with brands and products to represent a reliable target. The sweet spot was college-age guys aged seventeen to twenty-two.

3. *The money is in denim.* We learned it was best to ignore the "casuals" even though, at the time, the Gap was enjoying phenomenal success with its khakis. Clothing marketers are easily distracted by other lines of apparel. They are a great idea when you're hot and can build on existing business, but they're a terrible idea when you don't have any traction to begin with. Fortunately, the leaders at Lee knew that their core competency was denim manufacturing, and they wisely resisted the impulse to pursue something entirely new.

The meeting went well, but there was one hitch: funding for research. We all admitted that we didn't know as much as we needed to about teenage boys and why they bought jeans, but

Lee organized its budgets around product lines and not on the overall brand. We needed to conduct serious market research, but the product line managers were understandably reluctant to sacrifice their line's marketing dollars to fund general research. We were at an impasse.

Then, during a break in the meeting, our team members met in the hall. They understood that if no one did the research, this process would go nowhere. So the four of them decided that they would volunteer the agency to fund the research—about $45,000 from our own pocket. Technically, none of the Fallon team leaders at this meeting had the fiduciary authority to make this call, but Fallon teams operate very entrepreneurially. They knew that they were likely to waste more than $45,000 trying to work around the problem. It was better to take the risk and keep the momentum going.

Not surprisingly, Lee accepted our offer. Unfortunately, the findings from the research were discouraging. The only positive attribute that Lee could claim with any degree of credibility was durability. (Durability had two dimensions: the pants were tough and lasted a long time, and the company itself had been around a long time.) The good news was that Lee absolutely owned this product attribute. The bad news was that durability didn't immediately suggest a marketing execution that would work with young men.

There was one glimmer of hope. Through the research, the team had learned something about the emotional connection between teenage boys and their favorite jeans. The team used a visual projection technique where we showed our new target market images and asked them to pick which picture best represented how they wanted to feel while wearing their favorite jeans. Consistently, these young men chose an image of a man pushing a boulder up a hill. (They also chose an image of pro basketball great Michael Jordon.)

Through this exercise, we learned that these guys wanted to feel absolutely indestructible in their jeans. This was radically different from what women cared about, from the emotional ground we had tried to own in our previous work for Lee, and even from what many would assume about a product in the fashion category. For young men, how they felt in their jeans was more important than how they looked.

We had yet to turn over the planning insights to the copywriters and art directors, but the team was getting excited about the idea of Lee's "indestructible spirit." We began to think that we could reframe durability from a product benefit (tough) to an emotional feeling ("I feel indestructible").

Sounds pretty iffy, doesn't it? We thought so. This insight lacked the power of Purina's clue into why people were buying less Dog Chow, and it certainly didn't have the "Eureka!" feeling we got when we discovered balance seekers for Citi. So it should have come as no surprise to us when the research meeting with the client didn't go well. We couldn't blame them. After two-and-a-half hours, Gordon Harton, then vice president of marketing, said, "You lost me the first time you said 'durability.' I want a way to make Lee sexy, and you're saying all we've got is durability?" President Terry Lay was disappointed enough to observe, "This is a bunch of crap."

Frankly, both agency and client found themselves in unfamiliar territory compared with the women's market. But we were steadfast in our need to find a credible way to start the conversation with young men, because this was the only angle we had on brand equity. We had one more exercise worth trying: the brand iconography.

Cleaning Out a Brand's Closet

When a brand goes astray, we often go back to its roots. It's the ultimate exercise in starting from scratch. You ignore everything you currently associate with the brand and see whether you can find a treasure from the brand's past that resonates today.

Our team literally went into a closet in the basement of Lee's headquarters. During their archeological brand dig, the team members found a fourteen-inch plaster doll named Buddy Lee. In the 1930s, Buddy Lee had been displayed in department store windows to let people know that the store carried the Lee line of overalls. In his day, Buddy Lee had been an icon. (Collectors claim that in the early forties, Buddy Lee—dressed in a miniature pair of denim overalls—was the second most popular doll in the country, behind Shirley Temple.)[4] The team grabbed the doll and several other icons, slogans, and visual images from years gone by and took them back to the agency to figure out what we had.

The team presented what they found in the Lee archives to focus groups. They got a good response to an old slogan related to durability: "Can't Bust 'Em." But then something interesting had happened that the team wasn't sure what to do with. When the team presented the Buddy Lee doll, they saw a huge spike in interest.

As we've noted before, it's important to watch a focus group's energy level, but that doesn't mean you immediately know how to leverage the interest. The team was intrigued by the reaction to the doll, but they didn't know what the teenagers' response to Buddy Lee meant. These kids were growing up on a healthy dose of *The Simpsons* and *South Park*. Maybe

The Power of Iconography

When *Time* magazine appointed Fallon in 1991, obituaries were being written for newsweeklies like *Time*. During the first Gulf War, the news pipeline had exploded, and now CNN and other cable stations were delivering news twenty-four hours a day. *Time*'s subscriber base was at risk.

This was a business-to-business assignment. Our job was to create a campaign that would capture the interest of advertising media buyers. The challenge was to elevate the brand's relevance in a commoditized category that technology was threatening to make less relevant.

We started by examining how readers felt about *Time*'s editorial content. The key finding from the consumer research was that as the amount of news increased, the need for insight and news analysis increased as well. In addition, the strength of *Time*'s photography brought important texture and dimension to the magazine's voice and helped *Time* offer a nuanced and more complete perspective than other news sources.

But how do you capture in an ad something as ephemeral as a newsmagazine's voice and editorial relevance to its readers? This was where the iconography study came in. We learned that the red border on *Time*'s cover had a strong resonance with consumers. Unlike any other magazine masthead, it signaled importance and credibility and was immediately recognizable as associated with *Time*.

We started to see that *Time*'s differentiating position was the entire package—in other words, everything within that red border. So a veteran art director invented a visual expression of this finding. By superimposing the red border of *Time*'s cover on arresting photographs (that actually appeared in *Time*) the campaign visually represented the perspective *Time* brings to the events that shape our world.

The red border campaign was launched in 1994 and continues to run. We've produced more than one hundred ads to date. The One Club in New York voted it the print campaign of the decade. Thirteen years after people began talking about the demise of the newsweekly category, *Time* continues to lead the category on key brand dimensions. As Bruce Hallett, a former president of *Time*, said, "The campaign allowed *Time* to expand its borders, to think bigger about what we were and what we might become."[a]

a. Bruce Hallett, conversation with Fallon's *Time* team, 2000.

they liked Buddy Lee simply because it was weird. Or maybe it was nothing.

Because the team members didn't know where to take Buddy Lee and "Can't Bust 'Em," they kept this discovery under the radar. They weren't about to let some cool archival element wag the tail of the strategic dog. Bring a doll and an old slogan to a smart client with no strategic context, and the client will feel that you're spinning your wheels. We can't let creative enthusiasm overtake strategy—a mistake we made with the Miller campaign. The door to most businesspeople's right brain is through their left brain. First the smart, then the exciting. (The consumer, ironically, wants it just the other way around.)

Buddy Lee. Could a sixty-year-old doll we found in a closet go back to work as a brand icon?

The team needed to make the strategic case for Buddy Lee. They did a study of other advertisers that had used iconlike characters, with varying degrees of success. Remember Mr. K. from the ill-fated Nissan campaign in the mid-1990s? The Chihuahua from Taco Bell? Little Penny and Nike? The sock puppet spokesdog for Pets.com, which was more successful than the business concept itself? In the end the character with the most staying power was the Energizer Bunny; it has enjoyed vitality and meaning for twenty years. (The account planner behind the Energizer Bunny campaign at Chiat\Day was Rob White, now president of Fallon Minneapolis.)

The team concluded that if Buddy Lee were to work he would need a list of do's and don'ts to ensure that he would support the brand. He couldn't be a huckster for the brand, or too gimmicky. Buddy needed to have heart and humanity. The team was so convinced that Buddy Lee was a risk worth taking that they went so far as to propose metrics on how they would track his impact after launch. Feeling that our need for accountability would demonstrate how serious we were about this recommendation, we created an addendum to Lee's ongoing consumer tracking study that would be used to learn from the marketplace: Was he likable? Inspirational? The team covered every angle, all to see how nineteen-year-old men might feel about a little man doll.

At this point, the agency actually recommended that we create a whole new brand. We didn't feel there was enough equity in the Lee name to be successful in the young men's market dominated by Levi's. Lee president Terry Lay accepted the logic of our recommendation, but he explained that we had been hired to pump life into the Lee brand, and he wasn't ready to abandon that mission.

The solution was to create a subbrand to end-run the problem: Lee Dungarees. Taking cues from the brand's hundred-year history of making long-lasting, workwear-inspired jeans, the product designers did a wonderful job designing Lee Dungarees. The result was a classic five-pocket boot-cut jean made with 14-ounce ring-spun denim (the most durable denim in the marketplace) and the reintroduction of the carpenter jean, a loose-fitting, function-driven jean complete with a hammer loop and side pockets. Both jeans—through their form and function—helped reinforce the idea of Lee's "Indestructible Spirit." All the elements were finally coming together.

Can't Bust 'Em

On July 25, 1997, it was time to present Lee's new campaign to management. The team had integrated the Dungarees product line (where durability was a prominent product feature), the brand's "indestructible spirit" (as a guiding strategy that resonated with the target market), and the Buddy Lee doll and the "Can't Bust 'Em" slogan (as the iconography that would drive the ads) into one strategic package. We felt that it was all coming together, and it was all sharply differentiated from Levi's and the other brands in the market.

Now that it was all synchronized as a total new product launch, the senior management team could see Buddy Lee's potential, but as with the case of Skoda, they were unsure about the boldness of the execution. After all, the people behind the scenes see the complete strategy, but consumers see only the campaign. Would Buddy Lee make them a retail laughingstock? Would consumers really connect with a doll? And would this strategy and icon really move the needle? In the end, Lee embraced the risk because campaign was backed by solid strategy, and doing nothing would have been much worse.

Now the challenge to our team was to turn this strategy into action. One of our key insights about our young male audience was that "cool is having the confidence and courage to let your actions do your talking." Ironically, most jeans advertising at the time of the launch of Lee Dungarees featured laconic, sulky people standing around doing nothing (CK, Gap) or aimless slackers (Levi's "They go on" campaign).

Against this backdrop, Buddy Lee stood out in sharp relief. Buddy Lee, man of action, embodies the indestructible spirit of Lee Dungarees. Buddy Lee and his Lee Dungarees show that you can go anywhere and do anything. He withstands tests of endurance, character, and bravery. He fights evildoers, rescues small children, wrestles wild animals, prevents backyard barbecue disasters, helps the guy get the girl, and generally makes the world a better place.

The next question was how to reach the target audience. Malcolm Gladwell hadn't yet written *The Tipping Point*, but we were discovering what he did about how trends take hold. It was clear from research being done by organizations like Roper that the power of mass advertising was declining and that talk value (including the emerging phenomenon of "mouse-to-mouse" talk) was growing.[5] For jeans, the young male influencers represented only 7 percent of the market, but they influenced more than 30 percent of the volume.[6]

As with Holiday Inn Express, we needed to be tactical. The social stigma attached to the Lee brand required that we get to the majority by starting with the influential minority. These were the popular kids who were at the center of their social circles and who had the self-confidence to get past the Lee baggage. If the Lee brand could intrigue them, they would be fearless early adopters.

We knew we couldn't push them. They had to discover Buddy Lee on their own. We did a hilarious six-minute parody of a documentary explaining who Buddy Lee was. Actor Peter Graves narrated the documentary, and that gave it a Biography Channel feel. The documentary made no mention of the jeans; it was merely meant to provide a backstory on Buddy Lee. We ran the piece on Comedy Central at 2 a.m. after our social crowd was finished with bars and parties. To get our trendsetters to watch our parody we advertised it with

Seeding the legend of Buddy Lee. This is an example of the kind of small space ads used to build an audience for the "Buddy Lee Story." The six-minute "Buddy Lee Story" was then placed in environments such as E! network and Comedy Central, where it blended in with the voice of the cable networks' programming.

"tune-in" ads in fringe newspapers and used other assorted vehicles that built mystique and buzz long before the brand hit prime time. When we felt the clouds had been seeded, we rolled out to a more traditional media plan with spots that brought our hero, Buddy Lee, to life. As the campaign gained momentum, we developed Internet tactics: we used ads to drive our target to online Buddy Lee video games, where they learned about secret codes sewn into the Dungarees product.

Video: A family scurries to the safety of a basement shelter as a tornado approaches.

Girl: I left my kitty outside.

Video: Her brother grabs Buddy Lee and sends him out to find kitty.

Boy 1: Buddy Lee!

Video: Cat meows.

Girl: Oh wait, kitty's not outside!

Video: Storm over. Buddy Lee speared through tree.

Boy 2: Man, what kind of jeans are those?

Voice-over: New Lee dungarees. Buddy Lee tested. Can't bust 'em!

Lee Dungarees, "Twister," 1998.
Part of the magic of Buddy Lee is that there is no situation that is too tough (or absurd) for him to handle. He has saved a child from a runaway car; beaten a kung fu master in a martial arts showdown; and done some spontaneous DJing while being shocked by an electric eel. You can see this spot at www.juicingtheorange.com. Click on "See the Work."

Buddy Lee delivered. First, the anecdotal evidence. As you've seen with other campaigns, we got the pop culture boost. An ESPN sportscaster referred to one of the Philadelphia Eagles' running backs as Buddy Lee because the player was unstoppable. At spring break in Panama City, Florida, a Lee sales promotion team was busy handing out Buddy Lee T-shirts when a kid ran up breathlessly and showed them his Buddy Lee tattoo. After we launched the campaign we saw the price of authentic Buddy Lee dolls rise from around $100 to more than $500.[7]

The advertising metrics were on target as well. In 1998, the first year of the campaign, advertising awareness hit 40 percent and then climbed to an amazing 69 percent by November 2002. The sell-in to retailers in 1998 gave us the first clue that we were going to turn things around. Management set a high goal for Lee's sales force: three hundred thousand units, or double the previous year's. Lee salespeople ended up selling more than seven hundred thousand units.[9]

Lee's spending was never higher than 6 percent share of voice. This means that it never spent more than 6 percent of the total being spent on jeans advertised in the United States. Lee Dungarees, the subbrand created to save the franchise, now represents 25 percent of all Lee sales and has achieved more than twenty successive quarters of growth. And they are actually becoming cool. Measures like "cool to wear" and "for people like you" have almost doubled.[9] In fact, *GQ* magazine remarked in the October 2003 issue, "Lee Dungarees. That's right, Lee. They're cool again."[10]

Buddy Lee also had a cultural impact on the company. A new mission statement themed around *indestructible spirit* was etched into a wall at the company's headquarters, and each year

Closing the share of market gap

Given Levi's dominance of the market and Lee's image problems, these kinds of gains are remarkable.

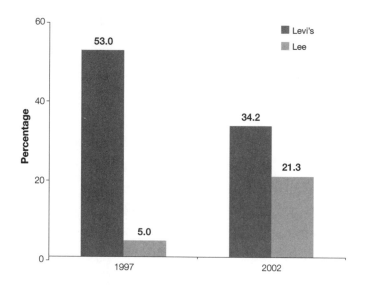

Source: NPD Panel data, 1997–2002; males aged 14–24.

it hands out the Unstoppable Spirit Award for employees who best exhibit relentless determination to complete a task. The award is—you guessed it—an authentic Buddy Lee doll.

Keeping the Faith

In 1997, if someone had suggested Lee could close to within 13 share points of Levi's by adopting a doll as a spokesperson, we would have asked for a drug test. But like the Skoda story in the last chapter, the Buddy Lee campaign shows that seemingly insurmountable marketing problems can be solved with creative leverage.

Lee also shows that seeking out strategic risks means more than making risk palatable. For creative leverage to thrive, you need to create an internal culture where teams are allowed to act on their passion for an idea. Even while people internally raised their doubts about Buddy Lee, the team never wavered in unshakeable faith that he was the answer. Like a sports team pumping itself up for a championship game, they imagined what victory looked like. And because they knew that enthusiasm alone wasn't enough, they were relentless in gathering the information that would support their idea. Instead of raising their voice, they raised their credibility.

Chapter Seven

Reenergizing a Mature Business Brand

Of course there's no question China has been trying to crack down on the Internet. Good luck. That's like that EDS ad. You remember that ad where these cowboys are trying to herd cats? That's the best ad I saw on television last year.

—President Bill Clinton, 2000

In 1999, the year Amazon founder Jeff Bezos was *Time*'s Man of the Year, it seemed that everyone was capitalizing on the digital revolution. Unfortunately, the boom didn't extend to information technology pioneer Electronic Data Systems. Left floundering in the world it helped create,

EDS was written off as an old-economy caretaker of mainframes that was quickly losing market share to faster, nimbler start-ups. Its slow, stodgy image was perpetuated by its history as a subsidiary of General Motors and its ties to founder Ross Perot.

In sum, the world didn't think EDS got it. The company was, however, one of the largest and most experienced data services companies in the world, with 120,000 employees and $20 billion in revenues. Somehow, in spite of the huge contracts it had with blue-chip companies, EDS had lost its voice in the marketplace.

In our experience, business-to-business enterprises face this situation more often than consumer enterprises do. Because consumer brands use ongoing tracking research, they can detect when their signal in the marketplace is weakening. A business-to-business venture, on the other hand, might not even know it has a brand problem. Often a B2B company with a brand problem will blame weak performance on the wrong issues.

Fortunately, Dick Brown, EDS's new CEO, had been our client when he was a senior executive at Ameritech, one of the regional telecommunication companies created by the breakup of AT&T. Brown understood that EDS's brand image needed a makeover. Even though none of the dot-coms was actively trying to undermine EDS's brand position, the net effect of the e-commerce hoopla was to make EDS seem obsolete. It's a branding truth that if you don't position yourself, your competition will do it for you.

We won the EDS account in June 1999, and our first effort to strengthen its image was a misfire. We rolled out a worldwide TV campaign that was, at best, mediocre. We tried to show that the company was more contemporary and more nimble than it was perceived to be—a legitimate player in the dot-com era. In a rush, we produced five commercials, Dilbert-like vignettes where managers uncomfortably face the complexities of e-commerce. You know you're in trouble when the highlight of the campaign is the line, "I thought we agreed to stay archaic."

This misstep burned up a big chunk of EDS's annual marketing budget, with very little to show for it. At first we blamed the ads. Nothing made these spots stand out—they looked and felt like a great many other spots on television—but there was a deeper failure. We had ignored many of our own principles for creative leverage. We hadn't started from scratch. We hadn't been relentless reductionists, nor had we found a proprietary emotion. And there was no big idea. Luckily for everyone, EDS was about to get a new executive who was going to put us in a sticky situation where creative leverage would be essential.

Is the Super Bowl Worth It?

In October 1999, EDS hired Don Uzzi, a chief marketing officer who had years of experience in consumer marketing with companies like Pepsi. As soon as this mover and shaker met his new agency, he asked, "Where's my Super Bowl spot?"

At first we were surprised by this question, if only because of the timing. The Super Bowl was less than three months away, and the dot-coms had created a sold-out market for ABC's broadcast of the pro football championship. And we wouldn't have recommended going into the Super Bowl anyway. The runaway costs of this extravaganza made it harder than ever to get a good payoff. The cost of time in the Super Bowl had doubled in the previous five years, but the size of the audience had remained the same.[1]

Uzzi didn't want to hear it. He was used to being at Pepsi, where his agency, BBDO, always made sure the brand had airtime during the Super Bowl. Pepsi had a ten-year history of having multiple spots in the event. But Uzzi wasn't acting only out of habit. He had a strategic reason for wanting a Super Bowl spot. EDS employees were tired of being part of a big company that looked like a nobody, and Uzzi felt that by giving EDS a public presence he would reenergize the sales force and give the company the clout it deserved.

It was a bold plan—bolder, frankly, than we were recommending. Somehow, through miracles worked by our media department, we were able to get commercial time in the big event. With no negotiating power because of our late timing and the dot-com feeding frenzy, we had to pay full freight for a sixty-second spot in the third quarter of the game: $4.2 million.

This seemed like madness, but then we reminded ourselves that Federal Express had launched in 1974 on national television. Why use prime-time network TV to reach the few people in the shipping departments of big companies? Federal Express saw the value of treating a business-to-business enterprise as a consumer brand. And it worked.

The campaign—produced by Ally Gargano, one of the hottest shops of the 1970s—announced, "America, you've got a new airline. No first class, no meals, no movies. In fact, no passengers. Just packages." Launched on a budget of only $150,000, the ads tripled Federal Express's shipping volume, to ten thousand packages a night.[2] By announcing itself as a

If You're Going to the Super Bowl, Make Sure the Whole Team Is on the Bus

In 1996 we created a Super Bowl spot for Holiday Inn. In 1995, the hotel chain had invested more than $1 billion to remodel its properties, and the CEO wanted to make sure everyone knew it. He told us to make absolutely sure Holiday Inn got noticed.

The spot was finished just in time to ship to the network. (The CEO approved it, but there was no time to run the ad past franchisees.) The ad opens on a high school class reunion. It's been twenty years since the senior prom and our hero is struggling to place the large, attractive blond he's chatting with. Suddenly a stunned look comes across his face. "Bob? Bob Johnson?" he stammers. "Hi, Tom," she responds. The voice-over says, "Imagine what Holiday Inns will look like when we spend a billion."

Fred Senn, one of the authors of this book, played tennis every Saturday with a friend who owned a Holiday Inn. After the big game, his friend warned him, "Fred, the old guard franchisees are going to get your ass fired for that spot." Fred assured his friend that most people would not be offended by the transsexual at the class reunion. But our franchisee friend was dead-on.

Even though "Bob Johnson" was one of the spots that got raves in the Super Bowl ad reviews, a few important franchisees were furious. Holiday Inn executives pulled the offending commercial immediately, and it never ran again.

Thankfully, the Holiday Inn executive team took the bullet for us and kept us on the business.

There are two lessons here about risk taking. First, to make the Super Bowl investment pay off, you simply have to take a risk. Second, there is more at stake than the TV audience that Sunday. You have to have buy-in throughout the organization to get the long-term business results you need to justify the expense.

brand as well as a new business, Federal Express also became a part of business and consumer culture, a position that has only compounded its success.

The Super Bowl started to seem like it could make sense for EDS. We certainly couldn't argue with the chance to reach a captive audience. Along with the Academy Awards, Hollywood's annual celebrity fest, the Super Bowl is the last, best example of a fading phenomenon: appointment TV, when millions of people sit down to watch the same program at the same time. For the Super Bowl, that means more than eighty million people in this country alone, many of them at parties and social gatherings where the commercials get as much attention as the game.

Even during a time when the power of conventional media is fading, the Super Bowl is still the world's largest beauty contest for commercials. There are roughly fifty contestants each year (in 2000, seventeen of them were dot-coms). Several publications and Web sites do immediate research and the next day report which spots were most popular. They also love to cast aspersions on the worst efforts.

This means that creating spots that will run on the Super Bowl differs from a routine TV assignment. Everybody remembers the famous Apple spot introducing the Macintosh—the Orwellian classic directed by Ridley Scott. (They've forgotten that Chiat\Day followed it up with an equally epic effort for the Mac the following year, a spot that landed with a thud.) There is no middle ground. You've simply got to rock the house.

Nice Idea but Can You Pull It Off?

Experienced art directors always keep a file of metaphors in their heads for just this kind of occasion. That's why we want people to be eclectic, to be idea pack rats.

Once, a veteran Fallon art director recorded a Jacques Cousteau TV program about swimming elephants in Thailand. For years, he tried to get the idea of a swimming elephant into one of his spots. Finally, he got the chance. Coke had enjoyed great success with animated polar bear spots one holiday season, and that prompted the company to ask all the agencies in their stable to come up with charming animal stories. Our art director pulled out that piece of film and proposed a spot for Coke about an elephant that delivers a Coke to a woman on a raft. Approved. It ran around the world and was a great success. To this day, it remains one of the most loved spots the agency has ever done.

For EDS we borrowed a metaphor from our work with QUALCOMM, where we often heard engineers compare the job of the information technologist to herding cats. Herding cats: two words that make people smile instantly. The phrase also expressed the complexities of EDS's business. This was relentless reductionism at its best: defeating the complexities of e-business is like herding cats.

We even had a concept in mind: we would bring the metaphor to life as a Western epic. We thought this was a big idea, but it was also a fragile one, and not backed up with the intense, rigorous strategy of some of our other cases. The success of the spot would depend on flawless execution. We had one chance to bring this cowboy metaphor to life in a way that would charm the nation's largest TV audience.

Every step on the road to effective creative leverage demands taking a calculated risk. When one of our creative teams locks on to a concept, we get out of their way and help them find the partners they need to bring it in right. Directors, music, voice—they know exactly what the finished product should look and feel like.

The creative team chose director John O'Hagan to film the feline epic. It was a gutsy choice for two reasons: first, the team had never worked with John. You usually like to go with someone you know when you're under this kind of pressure. Second, John wasn't known for epic spots or for special effects, two obvious criteria for herding cats. What the creative team really liked about John was his understated sense of humor. They hoped that he would keep a high-concept spot from becoming a cartoon.

The goal was to do a loving parody of the American Western film. The tone had to be just right. To give the director a sense of what they wanted, the team members pored over classic Western films like *Red River, The Cowboys,* and *The Cul-*

pepper Cattle Co. They also sent John clips of all the clichéd Western scenes: the lone rider poised on the panoramic ridge, the cowboys driving the herd into town, the river crossing, the campsite, and the big sky and big sky music. The next step in producing the EDS spot was to cast the cowboys. It was decided to use actual cattle wranglers from the region near California's Tejan Ranch.

Then the project came to a sudden halt on the orders of CEO Dick Brown. It seems he had attended a board meeting for another company, and when he told his colleagues about his Super Bowl plans, they told him it was nothing but a vanity thing, a mistake, and a big waste of money. He took their remarks to heart, and as soon as he got back to Texas he told his people to pull the plug.

A Quick Trip to Subway

If EDS was an example of lightweight strategy and sterling execution, then our experience with Subway was just the opposite. In 2004, we won the Subway account with rock-solid strategy, but lost it because we couldn't execute.

Using syndicated market research, we found a group of fifty million fast food junkies that visited Subway for one of their twenty fast food meals a month. In focus groups we also learned that people think about nutrition as a balancing game: they eat healthy on one occasion so they can indulge on another. Building on Subway's reputation as a healthy fast food chain, we surmised that the target market might respond to an invitation to "be good" at Subway so they could "be bad" at other restaurants. If we could get people to visit Subway just one more time a month, Subway's sales would grow by half!

The spots spoke directly to the nutritional balancing, but the problem was that we could never find the right voice in the execution. Our ads were too over the top. For example, one of the spots shows a man confronting his wife who is eating ice cream right out of a quart container. "It's OK," she says, "I had Subway for lunch." Later the man is washing the family car in a cheerleader's outfit. "It's OK," he tells his horrified bride. "I had Subway!"

Two weeks after the campaign launched Subway sales increased (after an eighteen month decline) and average store sales were up 12 percent. But our ads were too polarizing. They annoyed people. A mere nine months after we won the account, we lost it. A great strategy goes to waste if you can't bring it to life with equally great creativity.

It soon became clear that stopping production would be painfully expensive. In addition to the potential loss of at least a million dollars to dump the media time back on the market, the company now faced the typical 50 percent penalty for canceling production, a penalty that would cost several hundred thousand dollars. Stopping at this point could cost between $2 million and $3 million—and going ahead would cost more than $6 million, a considerable portion of EDS's 2000 budget.

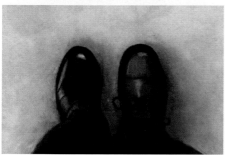

United Airlines TV spot, "Interview," 2005
This commercial has no dialogue. The story is well told with pictures and the famous Gershwin score. We see a man struggling to get to an important job interview in a faraway city. Walking into the room, he realizes to his dismay that he is wearing one brown shoe and one black shoe. Somehow he gets through the interview despite fearing that his sartorial mistake has doomed him. Back on the street, he gets a call on his cell phone. We see by his jubilation that he has won the job. He flies home a happy warrior.

We've all made stupid little dressing mistakes before a big meeting. What makes this commerical captivating is that the story is well told without a word being said. In each of these spots, musicians from the San Francisco Philharmonic recorded a specially adapted version of *Rhapsody in Blue* scored to the animation. You can see this spot at www.juicingtheorange.com: click on "See the Work."

There are people who shoulda, coulda, woulda.
And there are people who are glad they did.

#UNITED
It's time to fly.™

A STAR ALLIANCE MEMBER ✦®

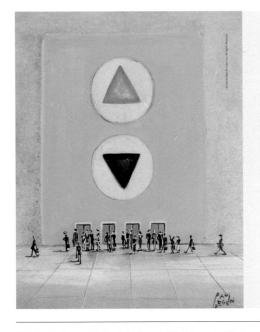

Let's face it.
It's hard to climb
the corporate
ladder without
going up 30,000
feet.

A STAR ALLIANCE MEMBER ✦®
united.com

#UNITED
It's time to fly.™

Print ads from United Airlines' "It's Time to Fly" campaign. How do you match in print the elegance of the animation in United's TV commercials? The concept was that these ads should look like the best covers of the *New Yorker.* But in this medium, we had to get right to the point and show that United was an important part of the lives and aspirations of its best customers.

You didn't get where you are by finding the most comfortable spot in the office.

It's time to fly.™

Business is a series of battles. We make the chariots.

It's time to fly.™

Every face tells a story.

Join the conversation.

The *Time* red border campaign. The *Time* red border campaign is a good example of the emotional power of iconography to connect a brand with its audience. This campaign has run for fourteen years. The One Club of New York honored it as the print campaign of the 1990s. (Our work for *Rolling Stone* won the same honor in the 1980s.)

At what point do science and morality collide?

At what point do science and morality collide?

The world's most interesting magazine.   The world's most interesting magazine.

At what point do national security and common sense collide?

Join the conversation.

We cover the scenes behind the scenes behind the scenes.

The world's most interesting magazine.

Man 1: This man right here is my great-grandfather. He is the first cat herder in our family.

Man 2: Herdin' cats. Don't let anybody tell you it's easy.

Man 3: Anybody can herd cattle. Holding together ten thousand half-wild short-hairs, well that's another thing altogether.

Man 4: Being a cat herder is probably the toughest thing I've ever done.

Man 5: I got this one this mornin'. And if you look at his face [pause], it's just ripped to shreds!

Man 6: You see the movies, you hear the stories—I'm livin' a dream. Not everyone can do what we do.

I wouldn't do nothin' else.

It ain't an easy job, but when you bring a herd into town and you ain't lost a one of them, ain't no feeling like that in the world.

We bring together information, ideas, and technologies

Super: In a sense this is what we do. Bring together information, ideas, and technologies and make them go where you want.

EDS
solved.

eds.com

EDS "Cat Herders," 2000.   From the opening shot to the last, this commercial is a loving homage to the great American Western, but with cats instead of cattle. The premise is embraced with complete commitment as grizzled men nurse cat scratches, brush cat fur, play with yarn, and then ride off into the sunset. The computer-generated cat herds are flawless, but what really makes the ads work, in addition to the cast, is the attention to detail that is evident in every frame. You can see this spot at www.juicingtheorange.com: click on "See the Work."

Island of Bahamas Web page. The new Web site gave the Islands of the Bahamas a competitive advantage. Prospective visitors could quickly and easily discover the Bahamian difference online. It worked; 2004 was a record year for tourism and 2005 was even bigger. The number of visitors from New York increased 28 percent.

Behind the scenes. Unlike the cars in a traditional car ad, the BMWs in "The Hire" took their share of abuse. No long, winding roads or glamour shots for this model. Instead, the films shunned the conventions of the category and adopted a visual approach that gave the new BMW an edgy personality.

**BMW Films, "Ambush,"
2001.** When terrorists
order the driver to surrender
his passenger, our hero
faces a simple choice: fight
or flight. Director John
Frankenheimer and star
Clive Owen combined their
talents to create a tension-
filled car chase that BMW
aficionados love.

Frankenheimer was per-
fect for this first film in the
BMW series. He had the respect of his peers with films
like *The Manchurian Candidate* (1962) and *Birdman of
Alcatraz* (1962). No one
was more qualified for the
difficult shoot than Frankenheimer, who had also di-
rected *Grand Prix* in 1966.
Once he was on board, other
directors of his standing
were willing to take a look
at our scripts.

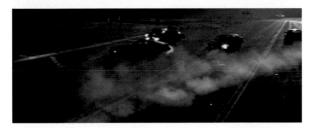

Virgin Mobile, "Snowflakes," 2004. Multiethnic musicians sing "We're All Snowflakes" ("It's OK if you're a Muslim, a Christian or a Jew . . .") in a cliché winter setting surrounded by familiar as well as offbeat holiday icons. The second verse extols the joys of Virgin Mobile's special holiday price and the delight of not being bound by a cell contract. As the spot ends, Tiny Tim struggles into view, carrying the Virgin Mobile placard, and then collapses in the snow.

Every network clearance department except Fox refused to run the spot, but the commercial created instant media buzz. When Virgin offered existing customers a free ring tone from the song, 440,000 people downloaded it. You can see this spot at www.juicingtheorange.com: click on "See the Work."

Our account director phoned Uzzi to lay out the options. Pack up, and we forfeit. To his everlasting credit, Don made the tough decision on the spot. "Go, but promise me we'll be in the top ten on January 31."

The project re-started just as the creative team was checking out of the roadside hotel near the ranch where they were casting. The weather at the ranch was bitterly cold. Thank God we had cast real cowboys and not Hollywood actors.

Under the able direction of our head cat wrangler, we had acquired all of Hollywood's trainable cats. The wrangler had

Long Before We Herded Cats, We Herded Chickens

One of our first clients was a local company called Gold'n Plump Chicken. In the Upper Midwest, Gold'n Plump was the only branded chicken sold at the grocery store meat counter. Their birds were fresher because, unlike the un-branded chickens in the refrigerated case, Gold'n Plump birds were home-grown and not trucked in from faraway Southern states.

The accepted advertising practice in the category was to have Mom taking the golden-brown, steaming chicken out of the oven and presenting it to her smiling family of four. We took a different tack. Our storyboard called for a war in which Gold'n Plump's hometown chickens—dressed in full battle gear—protected the state borders from the invasion of Southern chickens.

Gold'n Plump, "Army of Chickens," 1982. Minnesota chickens prepare to defend the border. You can see this spot at www.juicingtheorange.com. Click on "See the Work."

Another convention of the category was that you never showed a live bird. We could have animated the spot, but we decided to do the documentary version. We set up a stage with foxholes and little tanks made to scale for the big battle scene. (This was years before Hollywood special effects wizards figured out how to do all this digitally.) We found a "chicken wrangler" from the agricultural department at the University of Minnesota, who somehow got us our battle scene.

The commercial was a howling success for Gold'n Plump. Within six months, Gold'n Plump's share of market was up 13 percent in Minnesota. The spot got grocery shoppers' attention and added value through press mentions—all because this unorthodox idea was executed with zeal.

only two weeks to train the sixty cats for their starring role. All you can do with cats is to get them to run a short distance in a straight line toward a sound. One at a time, not in herds. These days, we would use special effects to make them do what cats never do naturally: run in a herd, with horses.

As soon as we saw the first rough edit, we were jubilant. We knew that this spot would play well on game day, the

Cat herders love their work. The EDS Super Bowl ad parodied classic movie cattle drives, with the message that managing e-business is like herding cats; a strong visual metaphor that is hard to ignore, and easy to remember.

question was how far the client would run with it. Clients always have a bigger stake in the work than we do. It's their money, their brand's reputation, their marketing goals, and their resumes that are on the line. In our own opening ad in 1981, we wrote, "Great advertising is, and always has been, created in partnership with great clients." That is never more true than when it comes to championing big ideas.

Creative leverage demands strong advocates. Sometimes this person is a soul mate. For example, John Felt, the director of public relations at U.S. West, had the kind of creative spirit you wouldn't expect to find in the plodding bureaucracy of a telephone company. Our work for U.S. West under his direction became a case history of effective corporate advertising.

In our most successful cases, our clients have acted as true collaborators to make sure a creative solution wasn't pecked to death by ducks. As the idea of the cowboy spot spread internally, our clients at EDS had to stay strong. EDS was a Texas company, and strong voices inside the company fought against the ad, fearing that it would reinforce the Texas cowboy stereotype. But our internal advocates helped us stay the course.

Showtime

If a B2B enterprise like EDS is going to benefit from a Super Bowl spot, then company needs to integrate the ad's themes into the entire organization. To make sure EDS's single sixty-second spot gave Dick Brown the organizational lift he needed, he rolled out the internal campaign well before the Super Bowl. "Herding Cats" was going to relaunch the EDS brand, reenergize its 120,000 employees, and help the company retake its rightful place in a category that had become hot, noisy, and crowded.

Brown and his executive team also did everything they could to make "Herding Cats" less a commercial than an event. One week before the game, Brown and his team put on cowboy suits and rolled out the spot to EDS's forty-five offices around the world via videoconference. EDS's PR agency courted the press, and the *Wall Street Journal* ran an exclusive story about the making of the spot, as well as how EDS was using this occasion to relaunch the brand.[3] EDS even released a "The Making of Cat Herders" documentary for places like the E! network, who were eager to hook on to the Super Bowl news peg.

We worked the pregame plan so hard that, in many respects, the client got its money's worth even before the spot aired. Every time the press picked up on the "Herding Cats" story, it not only validated EDS's rebranding efforts, but also helped create momentum for the sales force. And this was all before the spot had even aired.

When "Herding Cats" finally did have its one chance to shine, the spot was an instant classic. More than two hundred broadcast outlets and more than two hundred fifty print sources wrote about the ad. The *New York Times* said "Herding Cats" was "an inventive commercial that effectively made its point about the difficulty of technological tasks."[4] *Brandweek*'s coverage of the spot was titled "Best of Show."[5]

With more than a million hits a day, traffic to EDS's Web site shattered all previous records. E-mails poured in from EDS employees around the world. "Herding Cats" had returned the luster to the EDS logo.

Six months after the Super Bowl ad, CEO Dick Brown reported, "Our sales force productivity is twice what it was a year ago." A year before it would have been laughable to imagine an article about EDS in *Fast Company.* An October 2001 article (with the headline "How EDS Got Its Groove Back") explained how the behemoth had gambled and won the battle to reignite its sales.[6]

After the spot's triumphant debut, EDS treated "Herding Cats" with care. Many advertisers wear out their best work, especially when they are going after high demographic or business-to-business target markets. How many times have you watched a favorite televised sport, such as a Grand Slam tennis match, and seen the same spot seven times an hour? Our strategy was to use "Herding Cats" sparingly. We only ran the spot during events that had at least a double-digit share of the national audience, such as the NBA play-offs. Our belief is that if you're lucky enough to have a high potency ad, you don't need to increase the dosage.

As few times as "Herding Cats" ran, people had no trouble remembering it. Before the 2005 Super Bowl, the network ran the all-time most popular spots. EDS took second only to the wonderful ad where a kid offers his Coke to Mean Joe Green and gets a game-worn towel in return.

Having done what it needed to on TV, EDS now began to leverage its attention-getting metaphor in smarter ways. If you attended the Comdex show in Las Vegas that June, you saw "Herding Cats" on the Jumbotron at the Las Vegas Convention Center. At the EDS exhibit, you could get your picture taken with a cowboy who had actually appeared in the spot.

And the White House asked for a copy of the commercial.

Play to Win

Sadly, too few marketers ever get a chance to be a part of a history making effort. When we pitch a new client, we're always comforted to see someone who has experience championing big marketing ideas that paid off. Just as a sports team needs a handful of players who have been to the play-offs, a marketing team needs members who understand the hard work and commitment it takes to make the most of an idea. These veterans bring a winner's confidence to their team.

At first glance, the success of "Herding Cats" looks like a matter of execution, and the artistry of the ad was a key factor. But the campaign wouldn't have had depth without the support from everyone at EDS. Management embraced the metaphor wholeheartedly even before the spot went public; their PR people made sure it was a timely business story; the sales force made sure EDS's customers were in on the story. Their collaboration was essential. Our agency made a great ad, but the client made it creative leverage.

Chapter Eight

Choosing the Best Media
for the Message

The United States has arguably the most competitive car market in the world. No one spends more money on advertising than car companies—$18.4 billion a year—and during any given night of prime-time television, viewers watch more than two dozen car commercials, some of them back-to-back.[1] If, like our client BMW, you're a smaller player, it's easy to get lost in the fray.

BMW is a small company in the land of giants, totally independent and consistently among the world's most profitable car companies. BMW has less than a 2 percent share of the U.S. market, compared with 5 percent in Europe.[2] In 1992, BMW sold only 54,000 vehicles in North America. In 2005, it sold 266,000 vehicles.

BMW's advertising budget is just over 1 percent of the total spent by carmakers.[3] Still, the brand plays a lot bigger than that number indicates. In an automotive marketing landscape of "zero percent financing" and "employee discounts for everyone" and of cars zooming around sharp turns or winding through strangely empty mountain roads, BMW has learned how to juice the orange, thanks in part to how the company embraces creative leverage.

BMW has chosen to play only in the premium category, focusing on quality and not volume. It goes head-to-head with Lexus (a premium marque launched by Toyota in 1989) and Mercedes-Benz, made by Daimler-Benz (which merged with Chrysler in 1998). Customers who buy cars in this class are saying something about themselves; these cars are often driveway jewelry for those who know nothing about turbos or stability control.

The business challenge for a relatively small builder of premium cars like BMW is to make sure that it has an exceedingly strong brand voice. The company needs to nurture the premium image and, at the same time, own the performance aspects that differentiate its cars.

What James Bond Taught Us About Marketing

As soon as we came on board with BMW in early 1995, we were asked to launch the beautiful new Z3 sports car, due in showrooms the following spring. Since 1990, the Mazda Miata had been the only truly affordable sports car in the classic British tradition of cars like Triumph, Austin-Healy, and MG. But now, BMW was about to beat both Mercedes and Porsche to market with a well-engineered, sexy two-seater. And it would be priced right. The challenge for BMW was to introduce this car in America without investing $40 million, which is the average launch budget for any new car in this market.

BMW had already made a critical product placement decision. Properly fitted by "Q" with every conceivable weapons system, the Z3 would be James Bond's new ride in *GoldenEye*. BMW supplied prototypes to filmmaker MGM and agreed to cross-promote the movie in its Z3 launch advertising in the weeks before the film's premiere. This tie-in was the cornerstone of the car's launch. Our job was to come up with the ads.

BMW apologized for giving us this project as our first assignment. As a new agency we had to serve both MGM and BMW—two company's with two vastly different objectives and two very different cultures—not to mention the legacy of James Bond.

Our creative team placed its bets on moviegoers' affection for 007. Our story line was that all of England was upset that Her Majesty's favorite secret agent had forsaken his British Aston Martin for the German Z3. Our first storyboard had the queen herself distraught to tears because James had chosen a BMW. That didn't get far. The Broccoli family, which owned the production rights to Bond, were friends of the royal family. But both BMW and the MGM people loved the approach, so we were able to work around the diplomatic issues and still make the point. We moved the ad's venue to the House of Lords, where a member announces, "My lords, today we have news that rocks the very rock that is England. James Bond is driving a BMW—on the wrong side of the road." (To view this spot, go to www.juicingtheorange.com. Click on "See the Work.")

The Z3 had only two short scenes in the movie—90 seconds total on the silver screen—but the cross-promotion gave *GoldenEye* the biggest opening weekend in MGM history. BMW almost doubled its own goal for preorders. We pulled off one of the most successful launches of the year for a fraction of the $40 million we could have spent.

The partnership with Bond and MGM served as an important prelude to BMW films. BMW marketing executives proved to themselves and the world that you didn't have to follow the conventions of the category to launch a new model. On the agency side, we got a good whiff of Hollywood and saw how it might help us break out of the restrictive covenants of automotive advertising.

Driving on the Internet

By 1999, the campaign we had launched in 1997 to celebrate BMW's performance advantages had run into problems. Tracking research assured us that people's perception of BMW's performance was increasing, and sales continued to be strong, but competitors with bigger budgets were copying our style. Mitsubishi, for example, was using the same type of black-and-white photography, the same editing style, and the same musical formats we had pioneered with BMW. Our share of voice in the world of automotive TV advertising was still only 1 percent. If we started looking like the rest of the pack, we'd be invisible.

We needed something fresh. As we approached the summer of 2000 there were no immediate plans for introducing a new model. BMW's basic brand message—that it was the "Ultimate Driving Machine"—wasn't going to change, but we needed to stake out a new way to express it. The clichés of the high-performance automobile category—fast edits, wet roads, hard rock beats—were verboten. Fortunately, our longtime client, Jim McDowell, BMW's vice president of marketing, threw the door wide open and challenged us to start from scratch.

One of our creative teams working on the BMW account had just completed a big, complicated shoot directed by Tim Burton (*Edward Scissorhands, Batman Returns, Sleepy Hollow*) for Timex watches. We did two *Matrix*-like TV spots for a Timex model called i-Control. The campaign also included an Internet component, involving virtual trading cards of the villains and heroes in the spots. The trading cards were actually short action films that featured the watch functions.

The Timex work sparked a nearly unthinkable solution for BMW: what if we broadcast short films on the Internet instead of doing thirty-second spots on television?

The timing seemed right, but the idea also felt slightly beyond us. Everyone was flocking to the Internet, but in many ways we marketers were behind consumers in knowing how to use the technology effectively. Furthermore, technology was giving consumers more choices for engaging with each other, and they were disengaging from unwanted marketing, shooting the messengers and the senders alike. At Fallon we were holding intense discussions about how we could use the Internet as a tool for creative leverage.

For example, we couldn't help noticing the success of the 1999 Victoria's Secret Super Bowl spot. The ad's sole purpose was to drive traffic to a Web cast for an upcoming New York fashion show. Before the game was over, the site got more than a million hits—so much traffic that the servers crashed. The stock of the parent entity, Intimate Brands, jumped 10 percent that week.[4]

(Skeptics may roll their eyes at that connection, but how could Wall Street ignore the public attention gained by the Victoria's Secret campaign?)

For BMW, research showed that their target market—men aged twenty-five to thirty-five—was on the Web in a significant way. Luxury-car shoppers were increasingly using the Internet to research their next car purchases and BMW shoppers topped the list. In 2000, a full 85 percent were using the Internet to gather information before they hit the showrooms.[5] Our connection planners saw this as a sign that BMW customers would not only be receptive to an innovative use of the Internet, they would applaud it.

By contrast, television use was down in this same demographic, and BMW's McDowell was becoming increasingly frustrated by the inefficiency of television. An early advocate of the Internet, he had declared the fledgling medium "mission critical" for BMW years before. As far back as 1996, BMW had won awards for the Web sites we designed for them. A 1999 survey by AMCI, an automotive research company, ranked our BMW Web site first of forty-one automotive sites.[6] McDowell also made sure that BMW's Web efforts were not an afterthought. While some organizations were dabbling, McDowell made sure his company's Internet campaigns were part of the overall media budget, where funds were more readily available.

A Media Planner's Role Is Too Limited Today. Meet the Connection Planner.

In their 1999 book, *The Experience Economy,* Harvard professors and authors Joe Pine and Jim Gilmore advanced the thesis that your customer's experience with your brand is a part of your company's economic offering beyond the product or service. The experience has its own value proposition.[a] Our corollary theory is that how people experience your brand should be part of your marketing communications plan. As advertising evolves, an agency becomes equally concerned with creating experiences as they do making ads.

In 1999 we introduced a new position: the connection planner. A connection planner goes beyond traditional media planning to find compelling connections between a brand and its customer. The connection planner starts where the media planner leaves off. They seek out the places where brands and people meet in the real world, and then connect the two in way that is often more credible and engaging than conventional advertising.

For example, for Virgin Mobile, our connection planners observed that our most powerful medium was Virgin Mobile's own customers. Because these kids are highly social and constantly communicate with their friends, Virgin Mobile now randomly rewards customers with enhanced services like periods of free text messaging, or free ring tones—out of the blue. As a result they talk to their peers about how great their cell phone company is and, like Lee Jeans influencers, move the market in Virgin Mobile's favor.

Through a cross-channel research study we conducted on behalf of Nordstrom, we discovered that busy women shopping the Web wanted more than just product detail; they wanted fashion inspiration because, while they love fashion, they often don't have time to go to the mall. Instead, they use the Web as a surrogate store experience.

They expect that, like the store, the experience will be fun, uplifting, and an enjoyable way to spend time. That's why we are experimenting with ways to deliver fashion, music, and inspiration, directly to the shopper's desktop, in a shoppable format. And by choosing not to invest in the ever less relevant TV advertising, Nordstrom is able to do what it does best: cater to its best customers while making the shopping experience truly enjoyable.

A traditional media planner might recommend that a luxury car manufacturer should showcase its brilliant new coupe in *Architectural Digest*. We could place the ad in an issue with a readership study. We could pay a premium for better placement or match the ad theme to the cover story editorial. All valid counsel from a traditional media planner. The only problem is that every luxury car in America is doing exactly the same thing.

The connection planner starts where the media planner leaves off. The connection planner works to create opportunities in the real world that are more credible and engaging than conventional advertising. A connection planner recommends, for example, that BMW invite enthusiasts to a driving experience where they can push competing luxury cars to the limit and personally sense the difference, because the brand's karma is about the drive. That could force the advertising agency to divert money from the media budget to fund the event—as it should, if the brand experience is more effective than a TV campaign.

a. B. Joseph Pine II and James H. Gilmore, *The Experience Economy: Work is Theatre and Every Business a Stage* (Boston: Harvard Business School Press, 1999).

Do You Think We Can Get Guy Ritchie?

Once we started thinking about the content of the films, we were immediately drawn to the great car chases in movies like *Bullitt*, *The French Connection*, and *Ronin*. These scenes are riveting and memorable and, if you truly love cars, almost hypnotic. The team thought that if they could capture the exhilaration of a Hollywood car chase on the Internet, BMW's target audience would seek out the films. An emotional connection doesn't have to be profound to be effective.

The final concept was to produce five separate episodes about a professional driver who is hired to help someone out of a difficult situation. "The driver" would be the ultimate personification of the BMW performance message. With unassuming grace, he survives these impossible scenarios with few words and effortless motion. We actually created a dossier for him (a story of the driver's history and credentials) describing in great detail how he became so accomplished and mysterious. We would call the overall campaign "The Hire."

We took thirty minutes to explain the idea. Jim McDowell and his team took only three minutes to approve it. We were scared out of our minds, because now we had to make the films work. From theory to reality in 5.6 seconds.

From the start, one of the most important strategic decisions we made was that the films would stand on their own as legitimate entertainment. Everything about the films, from who was in them to how they looked to how they were marketed, had to be in keeping with the standards of a big-budget Hollywood production. If the films looked like the products of an ad agency, people would be turned off. Because we weren't broadcasting the films but inviting people to watch them on a Web site, they would have to be so good that people would seek them out. In keeping with this thinking we even turned the normal ratio of production to media on its head. We planned to spend 75 percent of the campaign budget to produce the films, and only 25 percent on media to drive traffic to BMW's Web site.

We believed that the best way to signal that these short movies were legitimate was to get famous directors. With the help of Hollywood screenwriters, we created about fifteen scripts and asked A-list directors to pick one. Most of them were intrigued by the Internet's potential impact on their industry. Here was an opportunity to experiment.

We also wanted to get the right actor to play the lead—not necessarily a star, but someone with some indie clout. Clive Owen was our first choice, based on his 1998 performance in the film *Croupier*. He had the right touch of gravitas and mystery, and the British accent added to the story.

Luck was also on our side: the Screenwriters Guild went on strike, so the best directors in Hollywood suddenly had holes in their schedule that could easily accommodate a short project. The late John Frankenheimer (*Ronin, The Manchurian Candidate*) signed on, and others soon followed: Ang Lee (*Crouching Tiger, Hidden Dragon*), Wong Kar-Wai (*In the Mood for Love; Happy Together*), Guy Ritchie (*Snatch; Lock, Stock, and Two Smoking Barrels*), and Alejandro González Iñárritu (*Amores Perros*).

Despite our luck, "The Hire" was so much different from traditional advertising we felt like we had started a new business. Fallon Internet experts sat down with Fallon writers, art directors, and production designers. Even though collaboration is one of our mantras, this was the earliest we had gotten all these different disciplines together.

For the client, working with A-list film directors meant giving up control. Having produced TV commercials for thirty years, BMW had developed a fairly rigid process. Every car scene was carefully staged and timed to the second. There were *rules*. The car never strays over the white line. Everybody wears a seat belt. Network clearance demands that cars appear to be going no more than the legal speed limit, or you need that annoying subtitle that tells you these are professional drivers on closed roads. Now these hotshot directors would control the shoot. The cars would get dirty, banged up, and shot at, as the adventure required.

Our experience with Bond helped pave the way. Bond's modus operandi has always been to wreck a few expensive cars per film. At first this was very difficult for the people at BMW to accept. You can imagine the arguments between the filmmakers and the executives at BMW: "The air bags should deploy when the car hits the ground that hard"; "But the script calls for Bond to keep driving." For "The Hire" BMW marketers were, if not comfortable, at least prepared for how filmmakers would treat their cars on the set.

Issues with how the cars would be treated weren't the only complication. Directors didn't want to follow the script; the films couldn't get past corporate firewalls during the testing phase; the client invited the editor of *Car and Driver* to be a guest on the shoot, but Madonna has a rule against press being on the set. Under the steady hand of Jim McDowell, the team responded to these challenges by developing a kind of fearless versatility. Collaboration—often associated with slowing down a process—was the only way to keep the trains running on time.

If "The Hire" were going to be a failure, it wouldn't be because we came up short on our commitment to the vision. The films would premier on the Internet, but otherwise we ran the marketing campaign as if these were legitimate Hollywood films. We ran ads in the movie pages and in *Variety* and the *Hollywood Reporter.* We produced TV spots that looked and

Going big.   Yes, it's massive, but the beauty of this outdoor ad for "The Hire" is in how it mimics the conventions of a Hollywood movie poster. These films debuted on your computer, but you'd think they were coming to a multiplex near you.

felt like movie trailers. We posted huge movie posters in prominent urban locations. If our experiment worked, then the buzz coming from Hollywood would give our little films credibility.

In March 2001, we presented a rough cut of the first film to dealers. Some denied the power of the Internet to change their business. Others were curious. Still others didn't seem to care either way. They had long waiting lists, and so "going dark" on TV didn't concern them as much as it would have if their lots had been overflowing with new cars. A West Coast dealer asked, "Is Mercedes or Lexus doing anything like this?" We didn't think they were. "Then do it," he said.

Will Anybody Watch Little Movies on Their Desktop?

"Ambush," the first film in the series, premiered on April 25, 2001. We started to get hits on the site before we went public, and that started the Internet buzz among film aficionados as well as car buffs. We made sure that writers who followed Hollywood knew about the directors involved, hoping that they'd cover the films without shrugging them off as just advertising. It worked. They were accepted as innovative little movies—legitimate entertainment.

For another company, the public's positive reaction might have been a victory, but BMW isn't so easily impressed. BMW is comfortable with innovation, but it also demands excellence and hates inefficiency. An engineering company, they measure everything. BMW executives wanted to know how we would compare the efficiency of this approach to a traditional TV campaign's reach and frequency. We had to be able to answer this question.

The Reviews Are In

"A decidedly unique movie premiere was hosted by an even more unique film studio at Cannes, world cinema's perennial showcase of all that is new and exciting. The studio? BMW of North America, known far and wide as one of the world's premium manufacturers of luxury on wheels, has entered the movie business." *Movie Maker Magazine,* Fall 2001

"Startlingly effective." *New York Times,* June 16, 2001

"The ultimate in new-media, high end branding has arrived." *Time,* May 7, 2001

"**** Thrilling." *Variety,* May 3, 2001

"BMW has struck gold." *USA Today,* June 19, 2001

"The movies kick butt." *News Media,* May 30, 2001

When we were younger and our clients were smaller, we'd say, "Trust us—this will be great." Today, blanket assurances are not an option. A creative idea never has a chance to become creative leverage if the executive suite doesn't approve it—every leap of faith must be supported. When we venture into new territory, we lay out the metrics so that the CFO can understand the risks and rewards.

The Internet, of course, comes equipped with better metrics than television advertising. The number of film views, the amount of time spent on the site, and the number of discrete users were available to us on the servers' logs. In addition, we commissioned an online study of film viewers (by Action Marketing Research, a firm specializing in quantitative tracking) to profile our audience and verify that we were attracting the right kinds of people.

To isolate the impact of the films, we set up a comprehensive "pre-post" study by Communicus, a highly respected third-party research firm. Before the films launched, we put twelve hundred current BMW owners and prospective luxury-car buyers through a battery of questions about BMW and its competitors. After the films premiered, we asked four hundred of those prelaunch respondents the same battery of questions. We wanted to see whether exposure to the films raised the level of interest among BMW owners and owners of competitive makes. This pre-post method allowed us to do two things: isolate those people exposed to the films, and determine the effect of "The Hire" on their brand perceptions, purchase intent, and plans to visit a dealer. The research had eighteen image measurements, and all eighteen of them improved both for owners and for nonowners who saw the films.

Given the high action content of the films, we expected the image improvements in performance and handling. But we were surprised by the lift in other unpredictable measures, including value for money, and, of all things, safety. We've seen this kind of effect before. Our conclusion was that if your brand engages people in unexpected and entertaining ways, overall favorability will increase dramatically. That's what juicing the orange is all about.

The Numbers

By October 2001, only nine months after the first film premiered, bmwfilms.com had attracted more than 10 million film views by 2.13 million people. More than half of these film viewers were right on target: BMW owners and "luxury intenders."

But because "The Hire" was an untested new approach to marketing communications, we also had to come up with new metrics. We invented the "brand minute," which is calculated

---

BMW/Fallon brand-minute analysis, 2001–2003

With every strategic risk we take, we develop a plan to measure results. The Internet's metrics proved ideal for comparing the BMW films campaign to a traditional TV campaign.

We indexed the historical cost of a brand minute of TV advertising to our target market at 100. We learned that the cost of a brand minute with BMW Films was 44% lower.

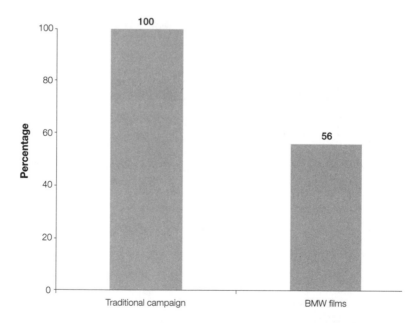

Source: BMW/Fallon Brand Minute Analysis, 2001–2003.

"The Hire" home pages. These home pages continued the themes of the campaign without interruption. We were in new territory here in 2001, leading people to branded entertainment on their computers.

More Branded Entertainment on the Internet

Since the launch of its site in 1995, Amazon.com has grown from an online bookseller to an Internet megastore, expanding its product offerings to include almost every-thing: CDs, jewelry, apparel, toys, tools, electronics, and even gourmet food.

By 2004, Amazon.com hadn't used television advertising for two years and had no intention to return. With fifteen million tech-savvy shoppers coming to your site every week, you don't need advertising; you already have critical mass. The challenge is to get your site's visitors to cross-shop more categories.

Our solution was to invite shoppers to think of Amazon.com as a more than a digital shopping mall, but as a desti-nation. We opened "Amazon Theater," a digital cineplex that showed a new short Internet film every week for five weeks, starting in mid-November. Each of the five films revolved around the theme of karmic balance. For example, in "The Tooth Fairy" (which stars Chris Noth of *Law and Order* and *Sex and the City*) a busy, distracted dad has to tear apart the house to find the tooth his attention-starved daughter has hidden from him.

In addition to the pure entertainment value, each story unobtrusively integrated a wide variety of Amazon.com products into its story line. At the end of each film, the products appeared in the credits, which viewers could then click on if they were interested in buying.

The idea was to broaden people's understanding of what the Amazon had to offer. People who only associated the company with books and music now saw that their site offered clothes, toys, and gifts. Almost half a million people saw the films the first week, and Amazon.com enjoyed the best holiday season of any online retailer, with sales that were up 30 percent.

as the amount we would have paid to expose a BMW prospect to a minute of television advertising. This became our benchmark. (We suspected that a brand minute spent on your computer is a more engaging experience than a brand minute spent watching TV, but we had no proof so we stuck to our formula.) We could now predict the campaign's breakeven point. When the number of brand minutes delivered by this experiment equaled the number delivered by a conventional TV campaign, we could consider "The Hire" a success.

Many people told us that we were crazy and that no one would watch films, by BMW or any other marketer, on a computer. The brand-minute benchmark told another story. Measured against a conventional flight of television advertising, the films were more than twice as effective.

After two seasons, we had reached more than fifty million film views. In the aggregate, between 2001 and 2003, BMW films' total cost (production plus media) of achieving a minute of brand exposure was 44 percent less than the cost of a conventional media buy.[8] Moreover, the seeding and buzz marketing generated enormous free publicity. Thanks to our public relations partners at Rubenstein Associates, Inc., in New York, BMW netted a calculated value of $26 million in free media coverage, and BMW was credited as having the "first-mover" advantage.

We also learned that Internet branded entertainment like "The Hire" had an annuity effect—the brand enjoyed the benefits of the campaign long after the initial promotion stopped. Even though BMW stopped promoting the films in June 2003, film views continued to rise. By the time BMW officially retired the site on October 21, 2005, film views had surpassed

---

The annuity effect

Long after we stopped promoting "The Hire," viewing of the films continued to increase, proving that we had created messages that people would seek out. In a surprising testament to the global power of the Internet, more than half the film views came from outside the United States, even though most of our promotion took place domestically.

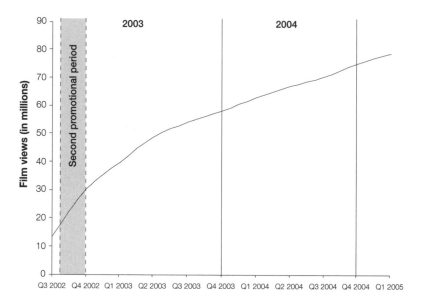

Source: bmwfilms.com server logs, 2001–2005.

ninety-three million. That's a lot of brand minutes with no additional media investment. Demand for the films continued to grow offline, too. More than thirty thousand people have gotten BMW's free DVD, either over the Internet or from a dealer.

What about the ultimate measure, sales? BMW was already on a roll when the promotion began. So even though we cannot directly link the sales impact of BMW films and the surrounding publicity, we can see that BMW sales momentum continued despite the absence of television support. In a year when BMW had no new car launches, sales rose 12 percent, faster than either Mercedes or Lexus.[9]

Kill your television

BMW took a risk that most marketers are now wrestling with. Should it take money from its TV advertising budget to invest in reaching its audience on the Internet? Despite a lower profile on television, BMW sales continued to grow.

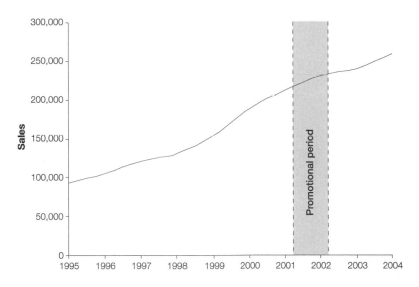

Source: BMW sales reports.

Let Them Come To You

BMW films are a good example of the power of creative leverage in this new media environment, where consumers are in control. The films worked, not because the Internet made them easy to see but because the team made them *worth* seeking out. Creative leverage requires thoroughness and commitment. There is no half-brilliant idea.

As we marketers head into these uncharted waters, collaboration will become increasingly important, as different disciplines are forced to work together. The challenge for creative marketers will be to find those touch points between a brand's identity and the consumer's experience of that brand. Our connection planners take us beyond the well-worn path of conventional media. But their new directions require greater flexibility, nimbleness, and courage as we get farther and farther outside our own comfort zone of traditional media.

Chapter Nine

Marketing a Network
of Businesses
Under One Brand

In early 2003, the Ministry of Tourism of the Islands of the Bahamas invited us to bid on its business. The Bahamas are an unusual country: a chain of seven hundred islands that stretch for almost six hundred miles. (The line runs from seventy miles east of Palm Beach, Florida, southeast to one hundred miles north of Cuba.) Only thirty of the islands in this independent former British colony are inhabited, with a total population of about three hundred thousand people. As the Minister of Tourism always reminds people, "We are not an island nation. We are a nation of islands."

In 2003, Caribbean travel destinations were gradually recovering from the downturn in tourism following the terrorist attacks of September 11, 2001. But the Bahamas were recovering more slowly. Whereas tourism in the Caribbean region was growing at a healthy 7 percent, the Bahamas' recovery rate was only 4.3 percent, and the Ministry of Tourism suspected the reason was in the way the country was marketing itself. Given that tourism represents more than 60 percent of the entire Bahamian GDP and accounts for half the nation's jobs, the livelihoods of most citizens depended on a dramatic turnaround.

The bid process was an official government proceeding held in a huge hotel ballroom on Nassau/Paradise Island. The room was set up United Nations–style, with microphones in front of each of the seventy officials who would review the presentations and hire the next agency. The stiff formality of the proceedings was intimidating, and we gave a PowerPoint presentation that too long and too complicated for that venue. Afterward we were politely informed that we had failed to make the finals.

A few weeks later, a small group of cultural ministers was scheduled to come to Minneapolis to follow up with Martin Williams, one of the agencies that did make the cut. The director general of the Ministry of Tourism had seen potential in our ham-fisted effort and called to ask whether the officials could stop by our offices.

In this informal setting, we got on famously. The stiff, bureaucratic tone of the official proceeding was gone; the government liaisons were animated, direct, challenging, and fun. In our impromptu presentation we performed better, too. We stressed that a traditional advertising campaign of print and television wasn't going to work. BMW films had taught us the Internet was changing the way customers gathered information on important purchases. If the islands were to restore the tourist economy to pre-9/11 levels, the Internet would have to be central.

The Bahamians left our office convinced that we were the only agency capable of a fully integrated approach. Shortly after that meeting, the Ministry of Tourism declared us the winners. Our new client was a whole country whose entire economy could rise or fall depending on our efforts.

The Unknown Islands

Once we were awarded the business and gained full access to the country's tourism experts, it didn't take long to learn that the initial challenge to restore tourist spending to pre-9/11 levels masked a deeper problem.

First, not all destinations on the islands were suffering. The famous beach resorts on Grand Bahamas and in Nassau were doing well enough. (This was good news, because one resort, the Atlantis Resort in Nassau, by itself represented 16 percent of the country's GDP.) But what are called the "out islands" were suffering even more deeply than we had originally known. Whatever solution we came up with would have to help everyone.

One problem was cost. As a result of their history as a British Colony, the Bahamas are somewhat more expensive than other Caribbean destinations because of their well developed social system. Another problem was more structural. Everyone was operating independently. Hotels, resorts, fishing outfitters, dive boats—there was no sense of common identity or purpose. The Bahamas as a whole weren't exploiting the power of the country's collective brand.

But the biggest problem was one of perception. *Rolling Stone* magazine taught us a key lesson about diagnosing our clients' problems: always ask about perception versus reality.

Perception Versus Reality

In 1984, after *Advertising Age* named us Agency of the Year, we got a call from Jann Wenner, the flamboyant *Rolling Stone* founder and publisher. He wanted us to develop a campaign to run in the advertising trade press to dispel the stereotype of the *Rolling Stone* reader. *Rolling Stone* did no consumer advertising, so this trade campaign would have to carry the full weight of repositioning the publication. And he didn't have much money to spend.

The problem was one of perception. Younger media buyers wanted to purchase ad space in the magazine, but their bosses who came of age in the era of the hippie counterculture, still thought of *Rolling Stone* as the newsprint bible of the washed-out and downwardly mobile. Whole categories of advertising—cars, clothes, and alcohol, to name a few—were rejecting the magazine outright. Agency media buy recommendations rarely included *Rolling Stone,* and its ad sales reps even had trouble booking appointments with prospective clients.

In one of our proudest moments of relentless reductionism, our copywriter solved the entire problem after the first meeting in New York, and he did it on a cocktail napkin before the plane landed back in Minneapolis. His plan was for simple two-page spreads. On the left-hand page, under the headline "Perception," was a portrait of how the media executives saw the *Rolling Stone* reader: a bearded hippie without a dime to his name. On the facing right-hand page,

Perception. **Reality.**

If your idea of a Rolling Stone reader looks like a holdout from the 60's, welcome to the 80's. Rolling Stone ranks number one in reaching concentrations of 18-34 readers with household incomes exceeding $25,000. When you buy Rolling Stone, you buy an audience that sets the trends and shapes the buying patterns for the most affluent consumers in America. That's the kind of reality you can take to the bank.

The cocktail napkin solution. *Rolling Stone* advertising salespeople were thrilled. Thanks to this campaign, they were finally getting appointments and selling advertising.

under the headline "Reality," was a portrait of the prosperous twenty-seven-year-old you'd beg to have as a customer. With the simple presentation of facts about *Rolling Stone*'s actual subscriber base, ad space buyers couldn't ignore the audience that *Rolling Stone* delivered.

The first, and one of the most gratifying, signs of success was a thankful cheer from the sales force. They were getting appointments. The second gratifying result was in the year-end numbers: the number of ad pages was up 17.8 percent. Ad sales revenues jumped 47 percent because the sales force did less deep discounting. Without a single change in product, distribution, pricing, or promotional budget, *Rolling Stone*'s revenues from ad sales increased by 47 percent.

What exactly is the difference between what a product delivers or attempts to deliver and how the consumer perceives it? As we saw with Lee jeans and Skoda autos, if you can address the fundamental misconceptions about a brand, then you can better figure out how to craft the right marketing message to close the gap between perception and reality.

The Bahamas were perceived as one-dimensional—a quick tropical stop for fun in the sun. And yet the country boasted an archipelago of seven hundred islands, with the clearest water in the world and a staggering range of geography, culture, activities, and personality. The islands offer ancient ruins, wild horse preserves, sculpture gardens, geological oddities, rare species of flowers and birds, medicinal springs, and historic churches and landmarks—most of which is lost on people looking for a sun-and-sand holiday. The true nature of the Bahamas was almost a secret, and that was the country's greatest liability. But before we addressed the perception, we had to know what the reality was.

The Factory Tour

As a rule, agency people dread "the factory tour." Not this time. The advertising team and the Internet team spent two weeks immersing themselves in the Bahamian culture and business (not without causing a bit of envy back in Minnesota, which at the time had a windchill factor about 100 degrees colder than the Bahamas). They were joined by a design team from Duffy Design, which at the time was part of Fallon. (Earlier, our design team members from Duffy had been involved in a Caribbean design conference. They were instrumental in getting us into the advertising agency pitch in the first place.)

This interdisciplinary team visited with people in every facet of the tourism business, from the fancy luxury hotels to a bed and breakfast on one island that was run by a charming Scottish couple for thirty years. The team first came to experience the unique nature of Bahamian hospitality. The whole country is like a small town. Everyone wants to introduce you to their cousin. When our hotel bellhop found out that Cat Island was on our itinerary, he gave team members his mother's name and phone number, promising she would cook a meal for them. Then he called Mom to make sure she was ready for them. On an enchantingly peaceful river on Bimini, our seventy-year-old guide explained how he had brought Martin Luther King, Jr., to this very place to write his acceptance speech for the Nobel peace prize.

The team came back telling stories about how well they had been treated. Touring the many islands and spending time with the hospitable Bahamians confirmed an undeniable truth that was at odds with consumers' narrow perceptions: this destination offered an amazingly rich palette of experiences that could broaden visitors' perspectives and leave them feeling engaged, enriched, and energized. It offered far more than strumming guitarists and cocktails on the beach.

Something else happened on this factory tour that changed the way our team worked for the better. Even though the members of this group represented very different disciplines—strategists, researchers, art directors, writers, Internet designers, and so on—they experienced the product *together.* The old marketing model involves research bringing the strategy to the art directors and copywriters, who then execute television and print ads, which are then translated somehow to the Internet. In the case of the Bahamas, the different aspects of the campaign all happened simultaneously.

Because they all started with the same blank page, the team members had a level of camaraderie and buy-in that helped them avoid the power struggles that can sink a complex, high-pressure assignment. Even more important, their early collaboration proved to solve the business problem. By the time the team returned, it had developed an approach that turned normal planning on its head.

The first thing they called for was odd. They decided the entire country needed a new graphic identity. The team had three reasons. First, and most important, the team felt that, in a sense, the Bahamas had never been properly packaged. A new graphic identity would give the entire islands a unified brand. Second, given the limited budget, a single visual language spread across all marketing channels would amplify the new brand. Third, for this program to succeed, the campaign would need to capture the imagination of the Bahamian people. If we won them over with something as personal as a new identity, it could serve as rallying cry across every island and every segment of business.

Duffy designers based the graphic identity system on the geography of the islands. Each island was abstracted in a different shape and color. Together, they presented a beautiful and colorful archipelago. The logo the designers created was both symbolic and instructive. We then used the logo as the basis for a highly flexible system in which each island's shape and color could be used individually to brand that island.

THE ISLANDS OF THE bahamas

Brand building by design. Duffy Design captured both the geography and the spirit of the Bahamas with this logo. All Bahamians felt represented, and the design gave the country a framework with which it could market its diverse offerings.

Once the new program for the identity was approved by the ministry, the team spent days presenting the new logo to everyone in the tourism business. A wonderful thing happened. That series of presentations was the key to mobilizing everyone in the industry. People saw the power of the brand, and they saw their role. It reinforced to the Bahamian people that their government was innovative—and working hard to help them. They felt, for the first time, that they had a point of difference, and an advantage. It prompted the individual tourism businesses to start thinking like a brand.

Experientials Wanted

To start, we knew that 80 percent of Caribbean visitors come from the United States, and half come from the eastern seaboard, but our analysis needed to be more sophisticated than simple geography.

We began by analyzing information from the Ministry of Tourism's rich database of more than four thousand vacation travelers. The database helped us define a segment we called Caribbean experientials (CEs). These were people who had been to the Bahamas, the Caribbean, Mexico, or Puerto Rico, even if only on a stopover vacation, in the past twelve months. They were active people who sought unique experiences, looked for enrichment, and wanted to try new things. People in this group tended to be affluent, spending their disposable income on travel. They were also influential—seen by other travelers as sources of information on the best travel destinations.

Talking with these CEs confirmed our worst fears: they simply didn't know much about the Bahamas. Most thought there were only a couple of islands (maybe two or three), offering only the typical sun, sea, and sand vacation. The destination didn't seem new, exciting, or appealing. (Interestingly, Europeans had already discovered the truth about the Bahamas' out islands because they work harder to learn about remote places. Having six weeks of vacation will have that effect.)

The overall goal of the marketing campaign was to change the way Caribbean experientials thought and felt about the Bahamas. Word of mouth and the Internet were the two sources growing in influence—at the expense of conventional travel advertising—and our investigation into the research habits of the Caribbean experientials indicated that, like BMW's target audience, they were ahead of the trend curve. We now had a clear mandate to make Bahamas.com be central to the execution.

Bahamas.com would be the most important connection between the islands and their prospects, but the old Web site was static and way too copy heavy. The team examined Web sites in travel, tourism, and entertainment. They liked the functionality of the sites for Disney and Hawaii. They were impressed by the design and color of Jamaica's site. But looking at the direct competitors, we realized that we could give our client a big Web site advantage even in the short time available.

We believe there is an essential truth about every brand that gives it the right to exist and prosper in the marketplace. The essential truth of the Bahamas was the range of experiences it offered. The essential truth of the business problem was that the out islands needed more support than the famous resorts. It was this multiplicity of experiences that we had to communicate.

This idea of multiplicities became the mantra. We chose "island hopping" as the theme. Island hopping wasn't the cleverest slogan, but, if we were going to help out the islands, this was a straightforward way to go. This stock phrase enabled us to showcase the diversity of the islands, the people, the activities, and the culture of the Bahamas. The island hopping idea also brought the graphic identity to life and helped shape the execution in other media.

Next, the dozen people now responsible for every aspect of the Web site had to build the content and organize its presentation. So they split into four teams and, with the help of local guides, visited fourteen key islands, participated in every imaginable activity, stayed with a Bahamian family, and shared a Kalik, the local brew. Along the way they gathered ideas on how to promote the individual islands. Bahamian people are intensely proud of their country, and they had plenty to rec-ommend for a Web site committed to showing their country's diverse charms.

The teams dutifully collected every idea on 3×5 note cards. They returned to Minnesota with a deep emotional under-standing of the diversity that the islands presented. They put up all the note cards on a wall in their brand room. (Every client has a brand room at Fallon; a small conference room that serves as combination clubhouse, war room, and work-shop. It's a place where competitive ads are posted, campaign timelines are tracked, and new ideas are explored.) The team began to arrange the note cards in various configurations. Where does this ladies' bird tour go? How about the aviation maps for small aircraft? Where do you put the docking tips for people yachting to the Bahamas? How do you cross-reference all the bone-fishing outfitters?

After two weeks, they had a workable schematic. Then they took a photo of the wall, removed the cards, and flew down to meet with the client, where they re-created the wall and the process started again.

Today the site displays 327 photos, but in the middle of the process, content was lacking. The Duffy designers needed new photography. For us this was easy—start with the bluest water in the world and then try to capture the love of brightly colored homes and clothes—but for the client the new art-work brought up an interesting challenge. What images do you pick to represent your country? Where we'd see a color-ful cottage in the country, they'd see an embarrassing third-world shack. Where they saw beautiful people on a beach at sunset, we saw a category cliché.

It became increasingly clear to the team leaders that between the client's desire to add more and the interactive staff's desire for better photos and functional perfection, the site was never going to be completed. So the client and the team agreed to a deadline of November 21 and swore the site would go live no matter what stage it was in.

A Record Five Million Visitors

The Web site launched on the assigned date as a work in progress. The design team felt rushed, but the end result was surprisingly better than anyone had imagined, and the Bahamians themselves were thrilled. The site showed the Bahamas they loved, and it felt right. They were proud. Now they had a way to tell the world what their country had to offer.

Beyond the new identity, the new Web site was so easy to navigate that you couldn't help digging deeper. In doing so you learn a lot about what there was to do and see in the Bahamas. Bahamas.com is a powerful tool, an easy-to-use, informative, fun experience that brought the "Island Hopping" experience to life.

Here are some highlights.

- *Booking.* You can actually book any part of your trip on the Bahamas Web site through a private-label booking engine. This was a first. It is also a revenue source for our client; commissions from bookings go straight to the Ministry of Tourism.

- *"My Bahamas."* This personalized feature allows consumers to save items on the site that interest them most. Then it lets them create a custom travel guide by accessing, sharing, and printing the saved items.

- *The Bahamas Island Hop Tour.* This feature allows users to have their own interactive island hopping experience. We used 360-degree Quick Time Virtual Reality (QTVR) photography, which gives people video-quality panoramas without requiring heavy downloads. Combining QTVR with interviews with local Bahamian experts in twenty-two locations throughout the islands, this feature lets site visitors tour the sights and sounds of these diverse islands. Visitors can experience the hospitality of friendly Bahamians, dive with wild dolphins, tour unique cave systems, view historical landmarks, go bone fishing, stroll through a native straw market, observe marching flamingos, and soak in the quiet of a Bahamian beach at sunset. Other features of the site let visitors navigate through the content of each island, including maps, fun facts, and the current weather. The result is a uniquely branded experience that is both lively and highly functional.

Having created a new brand position, identity, and Web site, we took the final step of spreading the word through an advertising campaign that included television, lifestyle magazines, newspaper, radio, and, of course, Internet advertising. Every piece of media advertising was designed around the new identity system and incorporated a call to action for Bahamas .com and 1-800-Bahamas.

In order to help the consumer understand the breadth and scale of the Bahamas experience, the team looked for ways to make a statement. At New York's Grand Central Terminal—the ideal place to reach millions of harried winter commuters—we decided to dominate the space. We bought several billboards simultaneously, each featuring a different island. For the print campaign, we bought multipage magazine inserts that were crammed with facts and photos that would tempt the Caribbean experiential to our Web site.

The integrated campaign helped drive a 14.5 percent increase in total arrivals to the Bahamas from January through April 2004, compared with the same period in 2003. Growth in bookings was reported by online and offline travel agent partners. The new Web site accounted for more than 3,600 bookings, and the number grew every month.[1]

The "Island Hop Tour" attracted 22,600 downloads and more than 95,000 views from May through July 2004. Sammy T's, a resort on Cat Island featured on the tour, experienced a huge surge in awareness and bookings (100 percent booked from February through April 2004) after the launch of the tour on the Web site. And the trend continues. For the first six months of 2005, the number of unique visitors to the site was up 14 percent compared with 2004.[2]

The Hon. Obie Wilchcombe, Minister of Tourism, commented on the international recognition of the marketing campaign: "In this exercise, we went farther than any other destination, certainly within our region and possibly the world."[3]

On January 27, 2004, the banner headline in the Bahamas edition of the *Miami Herald* read, "Five Million Visitors." The lead story trumpeted the new Bahamas tourism record, despite one of the most devastating hurricane seasons ever. The year before, the Bahamas had lagged behind the region's growth by 38 percent. But this year it had turned things around, finishing 28 percent ahead of the Caribbean regional average.[4] Quite a change in direction. If Bahamians can keep juicing the orange like that, we hope that trend will continue.

The Intangible Benefits of Collaboration

In a recent article in *Harvard Business Review,* Philip Evans and Bob Wolf cite not only the efficiency, but also the motivational effects, of collaboration.[5] They point out that monetary carrots and accountability sticks motivate people to perform narrow, specified tasks, but the psychic rewards of collaborating are far more effective stimulants for "above and beyond" behavior.

Our experience with the Islands of the Bahamas reinforces this lesson. Months before the country's busy season, the team was doing three things simultaneously: building a new graphic identity that would serve as the architecture for everything else, designing a best-of-class Web site, and creating a traditional advertising campaign to drive traffic to the site. Collaboration not only helped make these tasks logistically manageable, but also raised the level of the individual team members' performance.

BMW films and the Bahamas taught us to get design, advertising, and the Internet team working together immediately and organically. Because of the groundbreaking success of these campaigns, our people now view collaboration as an opportunity to do better than their best.

Chapter Ten

Rethinking Customer Engagement

S o far, with the exception of BMW films and the Bahamas, the campaigns we've discussed were executed mostly in traditional media. But every marketer is in a panic to move beyond traditional advertising channels. The business of connecting with consumers in the old way seems too expensive and inefficient. If companies with titanic marketing budgets, such as Procter & Gamble and Coke, are scrambling for alternatives, then surely the rest of us need to rethink our dependency on the thirty-second spot and the full-page magazine ad.

No so fast. The old model is not entirely dead. Some marketers still use traditional advertising very well. For example, Tiffany & Co. has owned a two-column-by-six-inch ad in the upper-right corner of page 3A in the *New York Times* for eighty years. Advertising rates have gone up and overall newspaper readership has gone down, but we believe that Tiffany is smart to keep its franchise position. The right audience knows exactly where to find the ad, and Tiffany keeps it fresh. It's not just smart advertising. It's smart branding.

Furthermore, the new model doesn't always work. In 1997 we teamed with Apple Computer and *Time* magazine to create an Internet experience for BMW called "Cyberdrive." It was a twenty-one-day virtual road trip with a different destination (and appropriately equipped BMW model) each day. But it was complicated and too high-tech for most who, in 1997, had only a dial-up connection. It engaged a scant thirty-five thousand people and left our clients at BMW wondering about our Internet savvy.

The key is to be strategic. In this chapter we look at three examples from radically differing business categories: an airline in bankruptcy launches a new low-cost carrier; a bold entrepreneur comes late to the cell phone wars; and, in an otherwise low-profile business-to-business category, a small electronic stock exchange takes on the giants of Wall Street. All three cases demonstrate new ways to use media strategically, and we hope they help start the discussion not only about how to use unconventional tactics, but why.

How to Launch an Airline with Friends Instead of Money

In the fall of 2003, United Airlines decided to launch its version of a low-cost carrier in its Denver hub. The first problem was that we were also working against the ill will airlines typically experience in their hub markets. The bigger problem was that United was in bankruptcy. We had a very limited budget, but given the magnitude of a new-product launch, the campaign still had to feel big.

United's design partner, international design firm Pentagram, recommended the name Ted (the last three letters of "United"). We sensed its power and were big advocates. In fact, there was almost instant enthusiasm for the name from all quarters—a rare event in the history of marketing anything—and the name energized everyone's effort. While United reconfigured and repainted the planes, it was our job to come up with a launch plan that would fill those planes with spring vacation travelers.

On the return flight to Minneapolis from the kickoff meeting in Chicago, two Fallon creative people went to work. These two veterans (the same two who created the "It's Time to Fly" animated campaign) decided that a guerrilla campaign, and especially one that was highly entertaining, was the best course. Because the product's launch was happening soon, there was no time for research, focus groups, or more meetings. Strategy and execution became one and the same: make a big splash, be charming, and make it happen, as much as you possibly can, for free.

In short order, the team came up with the idea that drove the whole program. Before the public knew that Ted was an airline, let alone a subsidiary of United, the citizens of Denver would meet a mysterious character named Ted. "Ted" would suddenly start doing unexpectedly nice things for people. We had brainstorming sessions in which we generated hundreds of ideas. The campaign would start a buzz about this mysterious extrovert going around town doing crazy, fun stuff.

Even though this was a freewheeling campaign, our account planner wrote a Ted manifesto to keep us on track that was similar to our Buddy Lee character bible and the dossier we wrote for BMW films' mysterious driver. Even when you're

Ted Brainstorming List

Ted sends flowers to people in local hospitals.

Ted buys breakfast for workers at a construction site.

Stop in at your local Starbucks one morning, and your favorite beverage is free—compliments of Ted.

Three bare-chested dudes spell out TED on their bodies at a Broncos game (and get free TV coverage).

Street teams hand out balloons to kids at shopping malls, courtesy of Ted.

All over downtown, pay phones ring asking for Ted.

Broncos' cheerleaders hold up a Ted banner (and get free TV coverage).

A handmade sign appears on bulletin boards at local coffee shops: "Have you seen Ted?" The sign has little pull-off strips with a Web address (meetted.com).

Ted delivers free pizza to the Denver 911 call center.

Once the buzz is going—skywriting.

doing something off-the-wall, you need guiding principles to keep the antics on strategy.

For Ted, the planner could have written a biography of this mysterious benefactor, but that would have been beside the point. Because there really was no Ted, the planner focused

We executed our "Towel Amnesty Day" mini-campaign for Holiday Inn using conventional ads, but it had the spirit of a guerrilla campaign. The idea came up at a brainstorming session while the team was marveling at a factoid: more than half a million towels disappear from Holiday Inns each year. GCI, their PR agency, came up with the idea: what if one day the company announced that everyone who had ever "borrowed" a towel was forgiven?

This idea was outside the marketing strategy we were working on, but the team decided to act on it because it provoked an emotional connection to our brand in its own quirky way: *you lifted that towel years ago, and you're still using it. It has that big green stripe with "Holiday Inn" in big letters, so it's hard to forget how it came into your household.* We ran a few print ads to seed the idea and put up a "Towel Amnesty" Web site to give consumers a place to tell us their story. Holiday Inn donated one dollar to Give Kids the Word for every stolen-towel story. The rest was public relations.

Twenty-five hundred towel borrowers told their stories online, where they reminisced about the circumstances under which the towels came into their household. Jay Leno and Paula Zahn gave the story national airtime. There were twelve hundred media pickups, far more than Holiday Inn had received when it celebrated its fiftieth anniversary the year before.

All in all, about a hundred thousand people participated—and they did so because the idea connected to

About the towels, we forgive you.

RELAX, it's
Holiday
Inn

For reservations, call 1-800-HOLIDAY, visit holiday-inn.com or call your travel agent.
As a Priority Club® member, earn points on your next stay.

All is forgiven. Ads like this one seeded a PR campaign that prompted thousands of people to share their stories of how a Holiday Inn towel came to be found in their household. The concept was a natural for news coverage, and the stories got more than their share of national attention.

their lives. (Isn't it interesting that journalists call these "human interest" stories? What would the opposite of a human interest story be? A story of no interest to humans, that is, a story with no emotional appeal.) Towel Amnesty Day proves that emotional marketing does not have to be high drama—only human and genuine. This is especially true with guerrilla campaigns, where small insights are best suited to encouraging consumers to discover their own connection with your brand.

on the precise kind of feeling we were out to create. We wanted Denver to be curious about its exuberant new friend. Random acts of kindness would be both disruptive and attention getting. The account team also put a framework around the campaign. They created a thirty-day planner showing exactly when and how long each activity would go on. The idea was to start with lots of small events and ramp up to bigger and bolder stunts.

Now we had to execute the covert Ted campaign. We hired a guerrilla marketing team in Denver. Our local Denver partners enthusiastically adopted the idea and even recommended activities that only someone who lived in Denver could have conceived. Our campaign kicked off on October 29, and our Denver partners quickly hooked us into the October 31 Halloween Monster Dash, a popular 10K race; our people in the crowd held signs telling the runners that Ted was cheering

Guerrilla tactics. We brainstormed hundreds of ideas, most in a visual form. Then we orchestrated the best ideas in a rollout schedule that let them build momentum.

them on. Our Denver partners knew the hot spots for morning coffee and the local charity connections for food and clothing donations. We learned the obvious lesson about guerrilla marketing: get the *local* guerrillas on your team.

Another lesson: you need an approval process not found in typical corporations. Our people on the ground in Denver were on the phone ten hours a day with marketers at United who had the authority to approve and budget activities instantaneously. When you have thirty days to execute the entire campaign, you can't waste a minute.

We started by having our guerrilla team hand out free coffee at all the morning hot spots, such as Starbucks. The first night, a crew showed up at the Denver Nuggets game and got a little free airtime by waving a banner that read, "Cheer for Ted." The media started following the mystery, and the street teams took the local event citywide by calling the talk radio stations. "I'm here at Starbucks in the Wells Fargo building, and Ted is buying everybody a complimentary coffee."

Once the local media took the hook, we got a local farmer to create a piece of huge crop art by spelling out "TED" in a cornfield. Within hours, the local TV station helicopters were hovering with camera crews, getting the story for the evening news. Now both the public and the media were trying to figure out who Ted was.

The "meet Ted" Web site got sixty thousand hits the day after the crop art episode. That prompted us to dial up the interactive component. Our interactive team started a running log of Ted activities, with pictures and press reactions so that people could follow along. The Web site got more than two million hits in only three weeks.

The final phase involved some paid media. Outdoor boards began to appear all over Denver, displaying twenty different messages. By this time the program had taken on a life of its own. The Denver media was having fun with it, and the story was even picked up by national press outlets such as *USA Today*, the *Wall Street Journal*, and *Business Week*.

We were finally outed by a diligent reporter, who discovered that the "Meet Ted" Web site was registered to the wife of a Fallon staffer. The reporter knew that United was a Fallon client, and he broke the news about Ted's true identity just as the airline ran full-page ads showing the new planes. The ads were headlined, "Be on a first-name basis with an airline."

Ted was a great run, with gratifying results. Ted, the airline, got off to a strong start. Travelers booked almost $5 million worth of tickets before the airline even started flying. Load factors in the first month were 82 percent, 10 percent over goal. Before Ted, United and Frontier each had about one-third share on routes served by both carriers. After only nine months in the air, Ted boosted United's share to almost 50 percent, and Frontier had dropped to 22 percent. (Interestingly, Ted gets 22 percent of its booking online—twice the rate of United.)[1]

A British Pirate Captures the Last Uncelled Americans

British tycoon Sir Richard Branson has made the Virgin name into a classic challenger brand like Apple Computer, JetBlue Airways, or BMW's MINI Cooper. When Branson decides to compete in a market, he takes on the whole category by rethinking how it's approached, especially when it comes to marketing. That's his—and the Virgin brand's—persona. And that's how Virgin Mobile succeeded in creating a vibrant young brand of mobile service in the United Kingdom.

In 2002, Branson decided to enter the cell phone wars in the United States, just as he'd done in the U.K. With major players like Nextel, Cingular, Verizon, T-Mobile, and Sprint advertising their plans relentlessly, the category is a lucrative one for American media—about $2 billion a year in ad spending, one-third of which is spent during the holiday season. Virgin's share of that spending is less than 1 percent. (Recall that BMW spends only about 1 percent in the automotive category each year.)[2]

Virgin was highly secretive about which agencies were competing for its account. Its staff had carefully screened the agencies not already aligned with cell phone services and invited only the most creative ones to pitch the account.

The brilliance and clarity of Virgin Mobile's request for proposal (RFP) struck us immediately. Here's the first paragraph:

> *Everybody wants the next great thing. Even us. So we are a music store, who became an airline, who became a soft drink company, who became over 200 different businesses all over the planet united by one simple common thought: We want to do what's never been done before. We want to create stuff that's valuable. And honest. And is worth making in the first place. We want to have fun while we're doing it. And we want our competitors to find us really, completely irritating.*[3]

Right away, we knew we weren't dealing with an ordinary telephone company. These Virgin Mobile people knew who they were and what they wanted from their agency. The next four-and-a-half pages of the RFP laid out an inspired business plan to take Virgin Mobile's user base from 500,000 customers to more than 1.1 million in six months. In our quarter-century in business, we have seen only one other RFP this inspirational and crisp—from Midway Airlines in the mid-1980s, after it was acquired by the same veteran Navy pilots who founded Federal Express.

Virgin Mobile wanted to see only strategic—and not creative—thinking in the proposal, which is rather like asking a talented musician to describe how she plays. The problem was that the strategic part of the problem was pretty easy, and the Virgin Mobile clients had pretty much figured that out. Unlike mobile service providers that lock their customers into complicated plans via service contracts, Virgin Mobile offered no plans. Its model was (and still is) simply "pay as you go," or PAYGO, as the telecommunications industry calls it. With this operations model, as a brand Virgin Mobile would have to earn its customer loyalty every day because its customers could leave it effortlessly at any time. Furthermore, Virgin Mobile wanted to get a greater share of the only "uncelled" users of interest—teenagers—and get fewer of the "glove box" customers who kept a phone in the car for emergencies but never used it.

All the competing agencies would undoubtedly concoct clever ways to present creative without "presenting creative." So in our proposal, we had to convince Virgin Mobile that we were the right people to bring its strategy to life. We created a coffee-table-sized "brand book" to show the Virgin Mobile people visually and emotionally where we wanted to take the brand. The very first picture was a puppy in a cage. The only copy read, "Let the puppy out." Next, a kid sitting on top of a building: "Be mobile-er." The book progressed to reveal a tagline: "Live without a plan."

Putting all our marbles on the brand book idea was a risky. A safer approach might have been a PowerPoint presentation about how to connect with teenagers, ending with the recommended tagline. But we were betting that the account decision makers would make a right-brain choice. Moreover, we were betting that we could pack the right imagery into this Trojan horse of a proposal to win. When incorporating such uncalled-for "theater" in a new-business presentation, you must gracefully enlist the prospective client as a willing accomplice. If it's too literal, it falls flat. If it's too implicit, it misses the mark. But we wanted to inspire these guys as their RFP had inspired us. And we did.

We won the account in early 2003. The first ads we did for Virgin Mobile were television spots that aired that June. Executing these ads turned out to be relatively easy, in part because Virgin had a strong brand identity. We didn't need much more strategy than that paragraph we liked in Virgin Mobile's RFP. The first Virgin Mobile spot debuted on MTV, of course, and featured a guy being grabbed by the balls—by his current cellular plan. Simple, direct, and very Virgin.

Later that year, Virgin Mobile gave us a more complicated challenge: to leverage purchasing around the holiday. As a "phone in a box" with no contractual obligations, Virgin Mobile makes an ideal gift, but we also needed to cut through the sludge of holiday marketing. We needed to do more than announce the brand; we would have to move the target market:

early teens longing for privacy, independence, and their very own cell phone but who still had to rely on their parents for "fundage."

As we had learned from our Lee Jeans experience, communicating with teens is tricky. Volumes have been written about Gen Y, but engaging teenagers is frustrating and elusive. With Virgin Mobile we had to be careful. We could have aimed the message at the primary gift givers—adults, a.k.a. parents—but that would have undermined the brand rapport Virgin Mobile was trying to build with youth.

In our research, young people told us that Virgin had a tangible benefit in PAYGO: no need for a contract. No bills. Good, sound, rational benefits. We could have stopped there and focused on Virgin Mobile's rational advantages for teens: Virgin Mobile's PAYGO was a welcome contrast to all the other advertisers in the category, which pushed complex and confusing pricing plans, bonus minutes, and time restrictions. But we knew that in this category, as in many others discussed in this book, a rational position is rarely sustainable. Those competitors that didn't already have PAYGO plans could add them to their offerings in a heartbeat. So again we went in search of an emotional connection.

We learned that Virgin Mobile had to talk with teens as peers, and not as a tragically hip parent. So we developed a strategy of "peer to peer" gifting. By positioning Virgin Mobile as the perfect means for young people to express their feelings toward each other during the holidays, we could make it their brand.

Thanks to Lee Jeans, we already knew that teens want to live life on their terms. Tactically, we chose to reach them during what we called "unsupervised moments," those times when teens were alone at home or in social environments with friends, clear of adults, free to be themselves. That meant buying television time during shows their parents would not be caught dead watching. By scheduling the campaign around such unsupervised moments, we stretched Virgin's advertising dollars, increased the number of teens seeing their messages, and reinforced the theme that Virgin Mobile was for young people, not their parents.

Most of our tiny media budget went to an area that some advertisers consider undesirable: late night, as in late-night network TV and cable (O'Brien and Stewart as opposed to Letterman and Leno) and late-night radio. All the people with jobs and paychecks have gone to bed.

Targeting unsupervised moments also meant finding social environments where young people hung out. We had outdoor executions in mall locations and placed street teams outside select Virgin Megastores. We separated Virgin Mobile from the big plan providers by making it the brand that teenagers saw as their own.

In April 2004, Virgin Mobile appeared on the *Cassandra Report,* a leading teen study conducted by Youth Intelligence. Virgin Mobile was taking its place for the first time next to Apple, Nike, and Diesel as a cool teen brand, as selected by Cassandra's cadre of trendsetters.[4] During that holiday promotion, brand awareness among teens jumped from 44 percent to 78 percent, and the subscriber base grew by a juicy 39 percent.[5] Given Virgin Mobile's low level of spending, the campaign's success depended largely on the entertainment value of the promotion and its ability to find traction in the youth culture, and not with media repetition.

So knowing that we needed a platform idea with enough entertainment value to attract media attention, we headed into the 2004 holiday season with an idea that would take advantage of the season itself. We created what no self-respecting assignment editor could ignore between Thanksgiving and New Year's: Chrismahanukwanzakah.

Chrismahanukwanzakah. Impossible to pronounce—or ignore. If you liked the concept, the next thing you needed this holiday season was Chrismahanukwanzakah cards, which you could get in both e-mail and paper varieties.

The word *Chrismahanukwanzakah* was not just Christmas, Hanukkah, and Kwanzaa mashed together; it referenced every faith imaginable. The TV spot, which was perhaps the quirkiest music video imaginable, features a band of multiethnic musicians and ragged holiday icons playing in a cliché winter setting. The jingle, "We're All Snowflakes," was performed by the alt-rock band Ween:

> *It's OK if you're a Muslim, a Christian or a Jew*
> *It's OK if you're agnostic and you don't know what to do*
> *An all-inclusive celebration, no contractual obligation*
> *Happy Chrismahanukwanzakah to you (and pagans, too)*
> *In some way we're all monkeys, well maybe just a*
>   *smidgen*
> *I'm a Scientologist, that's kind of a religion*
> *Whose faith is the right one? It's anybody's guess*
> *What matters most is camera phones for twenty dollars*
>   *less . . .*[6]

The executives at Virgin Mobile approved the spot instantly. An established category leader would never have green-lighted such a concept, especially not one that managed to offend everyone just a little bit. To their credit, the people at Virgin Mobile didn't care that every network clearance department except Fox's refused to run the spot.

The chutzpah of the idea and the delightfully offbeat execution gave the spot instant buzz. So Virgin Mobile challenged us to extend the story in nontraditional media and retail. We created a line of Chrismahanukwanzakah cards, both e-mail and paper varieties. Virgin offered existing customers a free ring tone from the song, which 440,000 people downloaded from Virgin Mobile's Web site. Web traffic got so heavy that the team quickly added new content to keep visitors engaged.

Virgin Mobile hit all its numbers and then some. Some 125,000 accounts were activated on Christmas day. Virgin Mobile far surpassed its original goal of taking the division from 500,000 customers to more than 1 million. Eighteen months after the brand launched in the United States, they boasted more than 3 million customers.[7] Virgin Mobile is still the little guy and has business model issues to deal with to insure long-term success—but they are growing and have found a place in the hearts of many of America's teens. The challenge now is to keep the momentum going.

What Wall Street Is Watching

In 1997, Archipelago Exchange, an aggressive niche player driven by CEO Jerry Putnam, began life as an electronic trading platform for professional stock traders. It offered all-electronic trading with more openness, greater speed, and better execution than any of its competitors. Soon it was handling 16 percent of all over-the-counter (OTC) trades, but few people had ever heard of it. Archipelago's target customers—hotshot young Wall Street traders—were hard to reach, unlikely to pay attention, and marching to their own drummer, not unlike the Virgin Mobile target group.

In 2002, the Securities and Exchange Commission (SEC) approved ArcaEx, as it was then known, as a full-fledged stock exchange so that it could compete directly with the New York Stock Exchange (NYSE) and the NASDAQ.

As with the aforementioned *Rolling Stone* story, the perception of ArcaEx was out of tune with reality. The SEC approval of ArcaEx as a stock exchange should have given the exchange more gravitas, but the target market didn't notice. As a result, Jerry Putnam challenged us to define ArcaEx not simply as an alternative trading platform, but as a real stock exchange—one that was, in his words, "unignorable to traders."

Everyone knows about the daily opening of the stock exchanges. The NYSE carefully choreographs each opening bell as a press event featuring one of its member companies. Arca-Ex is virtual: it has no bricks and mortar, no specific public location, no suit-wearing execs posing as "presenters." In short, it had a visibility disadvantage. So to play with the big boys, we had to change the rules of engagement.

ArcaEx opens at 8 a.m., ninety minutes before any other exchange. We decided to turn this fact into a competitive advantage. But our audience was extremely small, and reaching these people through conventional media would be both expensive and restricting. We could run ads in the *Wall Street Journal*, but most of our target audience was abandoning print as a news source.

Our media planners noticed that before the exchanges opened every morning, you could find a concentration of stockbrokers watching the business coverage on cable news. So we started from scratch. The recommendation: create a custom program to be shown on the right cable channel for this Wall Street crowd.

CNBC was an enthusiastic partner in this experiment. We created a sixty-second program to run between 7:59 a.m. and 8:00 a.m. every day. CNBC worked with us; our little one-minute bit ran alone every morning, never adjacent to other commercials. We called it "The Open Show," and it had a single objective: to redefine ArcaEx as an open exchange.

"The Open Show" wasn't a commercial. Instead, it was a one-minute episode in an ongoing sitcom about two guys traveling the world in search of the best way to open the day for ArcaEx. The girlfriend of one of our heroes shows up as sort of an uninvited guest. And as part of their search, they emphasize the benefits of using ArcaEx while using insider humor to poke fun at the big exchanges.

We promoted "The Open Show" as the big TV networks might promote a new series: with teasers and a Web site. We ran a contest for traders who wanted to appear on "The Open Show." More than four hundred signed up. Ameritrade invited us to film an episode at its headquarters.

There's a saying that good marketing can't make a ball roll uphill, but it can make a ball roll downhill faster. For the financial community, this electronic service's time had come. The enterprise had momentum because of its inherent competitive advantage—transparency. But the ArcaEx "Open Show" synchronized its brand personality with the hyperactive Wall Street types who were its target audience. Unaided awareness of the campaign was more than 50 percent, compared with advertising awareness numbers of 13 percent for NYSE and 15 percent for NASDAQ. ArcaEx's business quickly began to grow. Trading volume increased 54 percent between September 2002 and March 2003, and total market share increased from 16.4 percent to 23 percent.[8]

Before "The Open Show," only 39 percent of professional traders used ArcaEx. By the end of the promotion, that number had jumped to 65 percent. And more than 43 percent of professional traders said they made an attempt to watch the sixty-second episodes.[9]

By 2005, the electronic stock exchange technology was dependable, and it was accepted by traders. That fall, the 213-year-old New York Stock Exchange announced that it would merge with ArcaEx and combine operations. (That might have left us without an account, but in a shoot-out with NYSE's agency, BBDO, for the combined account, we prevailed.)

"The Open Show" was a classic example of creative leverage. A risky and unconventional approach to marketing communications built rapport with users and momentum for the business. This effort won the Fallon media team a Gold Lion at Cannes in the advertising media category in 2003. That year, this category had more than two thousand entries, and the jury awarded twenty-two Lions. Surprisingly, only two of those came from the world's largest media market, the United States, something that suggests to us that American marketers may be behind the rest of the world in when it comes to creative uses of media.

Outsmart Not Outspend

In all the cases in this chapter, you can see how the lines begin to blur between conventional advertising methods and the broader canvas we face today. Ted was essentially a rigorously executed grassroots guerilla marketing effort that only used conventional media at the very end of its run. Virgin Mobile seeded the clouds with TV advertising and then counted on the media buzz and the connectivity of its teenage audience to spread the message. Much like Holiday Inn's Towel Amnesty Day event, which used only a few print ads to get the PR buzz going, ArcaEx created its own media counterpoint to the traditional exchange opening ceremony, and did so in a way that engaged stock traders on their own terms.

What do these stories have in common? It's more than that these campaigns transcended traditional advertising. The unifying theme is that the job was bigger than the budget. As necessity forces marketers to be more creative, the emphasis will shift even more to the quality of the idea and not the budget. Share of market no longer depends on share of voice.

Chapter Eleven

Lessons Learned

It is a very grave mistake to think that the enjoyment
of seeing and searching can be promoted by means of
coercion and a sense of duty.

—*Albert Einstein*

Before we launched our agency, we ran a little moonlighting operation called Lunch Hour Limited with Tom McElligott and Ron Anderson, a wonderful creative director at Bozell Jacobs. What struck us was how effortlessly, quickly, and completely we could leverage our creativity outside the confines of our respective offices. Lunch Hour Limited enabled us to do the kind of high profile creative work that excited us but that would never see the light of day at our regular day jobs.

We realized that if we could escape the workplace politics, the bureaucracy, and the paranoia wafting through the typical ad agency, then we could unleash tremendous passion and energy. This meant building a culture that would allow people to consistently deliver actionable creativity from every corner of the organization.

We envisioned an environment where people could do the best work of their careers, and where we as managers would clear away all the institutional and interpersonal bullshit. We would team employees with partners who could nurture their talents, and we would fight like hell to bring a team's work to life. In exchange, our employees would agree to collaborate closely and to embrace creativity in all aspects of their work. We believed we could offer an environment where compromise was the exception, not the rule. That was the social contract we wanted to offer our employees.

We figured that if we were hungry to work at such a place, then other like-minded souls might be hungry to work there as well. Even in Minnesota. To flesh out this idea, we met many times at the Original Pancake House in Edina, Minnesota. After much deliberation and many cups of coffee, in February 1981 we agreed upon the following list of founding principles:

- The single-minded devotion to, and the belief in, the power of creativity

- The belief in family as a business model

- Seeing risk taking as a friend

- Success as a business imperative

- The importance of remaining humble

- The necessity of having fun

To fund the operation, each of us gave $20,000 to Irv Fish, our designated chief financial officer. Instead of a salary, Irv gave each of us only enough to cover our monthly household expenses. Our egalitarian drive was almost ridiculous. At our office above Peter's Grill, we had no janitor or snow shoveling service. Irv posted the rotating roster of maintenance and cleaning duties every week, and we took turns doing the chores like we were roommates fresh out of college.

We agonized over every hire at every level, in terms of both skill set and cultural fit. We wanted diversity of thinking, but at the same time, we wanted people with a sense of what's possible.

Despite all the grunt work, the dream was coming true. A short two years after we first opened our doors *Advertising Age* named us agency of the year. *Rolling Stone* and the *Wall Street Journal* and other national accounts started seeking us out. As for our culture experiment, we knew we were getting it right when the word spread that our agency was a place where you could do the best work of your career. We started recruiting over our heads, hiring people away from New York firms even though we couldn't pay a competitive salary. The work would be its own reward.

As we expanded from five to fifty to one hundred employees, our once-effortless culture grew proportionately more difficult to sustain. Some of the changes brought on by the increase in headcount were small. Pat remembers when he had to stop sending out handwritten notes to staff during company anniversaries. Other changes jeopardized the work. Directives

Organizational Changes Don't Have to Be Cultural Changes

In the 1980s there was tremendous consolidation in our industry, and we were not immune. In 1988, a New York agency, Scali McCabe and Sloves, took a majority owner-ship position in our agency. We'd studied creative organi-zations before founding ours, and we thought Scali had done it right. These guys were our heroes, and so we were flattered when they came calling. However, Scali was al-ready a part of Ogilvy & Mather, which was later to be ac-quired by Martin Sorrell's WPP Group in London. As far as global players went, we were still a farm team.

Why did we sell? At the time, we felt we had only two strategic options: become a global player, or remain a local player. There was nothing in between. If we didn't align ourselves with one of the big global networks, we would never play in the big leagues, and we desperately wanted to prove ourselves on a global scale. But soon WPP's stock began to fall. We started getting memos from New York driven by London instructing us to cut costs, postpone salary increases, and send more money to London—in ef-fect, contaminating our culture. So we proposed to WPP chairman Martin Sorrell that we buy ourselves back in a leveraged buyout. He needed the cash and so he agreed, probably believing that it would never happen. But we were determined; we borrowed as much money as we could, pledged our homes as collateral, and, in 1992, were independent again. Still a not a global player, but at least a free agent.

In 1999, Maurice Levy, chairman of the French advertising agency Publicis, approached us. We liked him, but we weren't ready to report to anyone again. Six months later, Levy returned with a strong pitch. He knew we still wanted a global profile, and we were feeling our lack of international clout. Clients like United Airlines, Citibank, Nestlé's Purina, and BMW all wanted our support in their other markets. Levy pointed out that none of us would live long enough to finance an international network on our own, whereas we could begin leveraging his robust global networks almost immediately. Most importantly, he offered us a level of autonomy that we hadn't had with WPP. So we sold ourselves to Publicis.

People ask whether our second change in ownership affected our culture. The answer, surprisingly, is not as much as you might think. To be honest, we're fairly certain our people would rather work for an independent company and not be part of a conglomerate, but as long as we continue to be ourselves and challenge ourselves, our employees are happy. Maurice supports this idea of remaining "emotionally independent."

became games of telephone, and we could no longer assume that important cultural messages were reaching every employee. Worse, departments began to compete with each other rather than the real competitors. Fostering a creative culture was once effortless; now we needed to fight for it.

Culture Forces Hard Choices

When we wrote down the value "the belief in family as business model," we didn't realize how much work it would be to protect that family. In 1991, we won Northwest Airlines' business. It was our largest account. We knew its reputation as a difficult client, but we couldn't know how it would threaten our culture.

Our top client contact at Northwest was creative and especially well connected in the music world. He was domineering and indecisive, a bad combination. At one moment he'd tell us our concepts were hopelessly inept. The next moment the same concepts were brilliant. The relationship between us and Northwest quickly became a battleground. We're not thin-skinned. The team understood very well how much revenue this account generated, but try as they might, they couldn't deliver work that both made them proud and pleased the client. As the client bullied the team and undermined their efforts, we realized that as managers we weren't sustaining the social contract we had with our employees. Fear set in.

We realized that if we didn't fix this situation, we would be fostering exactly the kind of toxic atmosphere we had set out to avoid. Good people would leave, and we would undermine our culture. Fortunately, Irv Fish, our CFO and founding partner, cared as much about our culture as he did about the numbers. One day the management team agreed secretly that we would resign Northwest—which represented 23 percent of our revenues and an even larger portion of our profit—as soon as we could raise enough new business to avoid layoffs.

It took six months to generate enough new business to make up for the Northwest account. We didn't replace all the profits, but we picked up enough small accounts to cover the losses in payroll. As soon as we hit our target, we resigned Northwest Airlines.

Financially this decision was a loss, but we proved to ourselves and our staff that we would protect our culture and put our people first, regardless of the consequences. The staff was relieved. Even though some mourned the loss of a big account, the decision was a quiet confirmation of why people had come to work here in the first place. We had made it through a difficult time with our mission intact, and at that point many became not just employees, but zealots.

Culture over Short-Term Revenue, Part 2

In 1995, the year following the Northwest resignation we grew 21 percent, well past our size and profitability with Northwest. This confirmed that our culture was indeed a strategic advantage worthy of defending, a belief that would be confirmed several years later when we were once again forced to choose between the long-term health of our company and a short-term gain.

In 1997, Domino's Pizza invited us to Ann Arbor, Michigan, to pitch for the account. If we won the business, Domino's would become our largest client, and so we pitched as hard as we knew how. In the final round, we presented our ideas to a roomful of franchisees, senior marketing managers, and board members. Usually high-stakes pitches like these drag on and on, but less than a week after our presentation, the client told us we'd won. We needed only to meet the chairman to close the deal.

Domino's chairman Tom Monaghan had built the business from nothing into a fast-food powerhouse, becoming a wealthy entrepreneur whose collections spanned Frank Lloyd Wright memorabilia, classic cars, and the Detroit Tigers, which had won the World Series under his ownership.

Monaghan was an orphan raised by the Catholic Church, and his relationship to his religion influenced all his personal and business decisions. So Pat Fallon, one of the authors of this book, flew to Ann Arbor for the "pre-Tom" meeting so that he would be prepared for their eventual meeting. Pat was told by their director of marketing that Monaghan loved our work and wanted to hire us. "But there's a problem," he said. "It's about the Children's Defense Fund. If you lose them as a client then we've got a deal."

It seems Monaghan had seen our reel and didn't like this pro bono client of twelve years. Monaghan's people told us that our association with the liberal CDF troubled him. At first, we took this as their code for a concern about a possible

Children's Defense Fund

The Children's Defense Fund is the preeminent American voice protecting the rights of children. Marian Wright Edelman, founder of the Children's Defense Fund, first contacted us in 1987. Her marketing director, Maggie Williams, had decided that CDF needed to raise its profile, and after studying the creative award books, she advised Marian to call us.[a] Because we preferred to help local charities, we said no several times. Marian was persistent. Her vision for how to help children inspired us (and continues to do so) so we signed on. For almost two decades we

AN EXTRA SEVEN POUNDS COULD KEEP YOU OFF THE FOOTBALL TEAM.

Become a father before you're ready and you may always wonder what else you could have been.
THE CHILDREN'S DEFENSE FUND

IT'S LIKE BEING GROUNDED FOR EIGHTEEN YEARS.

Having a baby when you're a teenager can do more than just take away your freedom, it can take away your dreams.
THE CHILDREN'S DEFENSE FUND

IF YOU'RE EMBARRASSED BY A PIMPLE TRY EXPLAINING THIS.

Being a teenager is tough enough. Why make things more difficult by becoming a mother too?
THE CHILDREN'S DEFENSE FUND

Fighting teenage pregnancy. A series of school posters for CDF. Sales of the posters funded the production of new work for a decade.

have done some remarkably effective work on children's issues, which is a great source of pride for our people, regardless of their politics.

a. Maggie Williams went on to become Hillary Rodham Clinton's White House Chief of Staff.

pro-choice position by CDF. But CDF has always been very careful not to take a position on the abortion issue. We even got someone from the National Council of Catholic Bishops in Washington to call the marketing director and clarify CDF's stand. Monaghan wasn't swayed. Domino's gave us an ultimatum: resign CDF (for which we got paid nothing) and get Domino's business (for which we would have earned around $7 million a year in fee income).

After we received this ultimatum we held what turned out to be a very short meeting in Pat Fallon's office. Bill Westbrook, our president and creative director at the time, said, "I don't want it on my tombstone that 'He stopped helping kids so he could sell more pizza.'" We declined the business.

Culture can be a strategic advantage, but the choices and the actions required to preserve and nurture that culture are rarely easy. There would have been nothing unethical or morally wrong about resigning CDF. Agencies "trade up" all the time. CDF could easily have found eager and talented agencies to support it. But the signal to our staff would have been chilling. Using our communications skills to advance children's issues is a long-term and deeply held commitment. As a result our staff holds us to a higher standard.

Identify and Encourage the Culture Players

It didn't take long to learn that if we truly valued our culture, then it wasn't enough to hire brains and talent. We had to cherish the people who best embodied our ideals. We call them culture players. If you took the person described by Ed Keller and Jon Barry in *The Influentials*—the person who knows in his heart he can make a difference—and crossed him with Malcolm Gladwell's "connectors" in *The Tipping Point,* you'd have a culture player.[1]

In our company, culture players know everyone and know a great deal (perhaps too much) about everyone. They are outgoing and optimistic problem solvers who treat every one of us with the same loving irreverence. Not all are managers. We put at least one culture player on every high-pressure new-business team; make sure they are there to train in new employees; and scatter their offices on every floor along the main traffic routes to help manage the energy of the place.

In our work for Lee Jeans, the culture players volunteered to fund the market research needed to crack the business problem; they didn't wait for orders from Fallon headquarters. In the Bahamas case, the culture players sparked the intense collaboration between very different disciplines. You can never underestimate the effects that a culture player can have on your business. We're not talking about the touchy feely stuff. We're talking bottom line.

Often a culture player makes a small gesture that can seriously affect an organization's resilience. In 2001, we were struggling financially. We had miscalculated the severity of the economic downturn and the dot-com bust. After twenty years without a layoff, we went through three cuts to align head count with declining revenue. As the holidays approached, we froze salaries and even canceled the holiday party. We couldn't afford the usual lavish bash and thought that a modest party would send the wrong signal.

Culture players seem to have a secret manual that tells them what to do when management is paralyzed. A week after the cancellation, two culture players (both were project managers) organized an unofficial holiday party. The announcement, made in a companywide e-mail, proclaimed that we didn't need jumbo shrimp and an open bar to have a party. They had rented the basement of a bar near the office. Ten-dollar cover and a cash bar.

By all measures, it was a great party. Thank God for the culture players, who knew that our management's hands were tied and sensed that the agency needed to blow off some steam. We have come to treasure the people who strengthen the culture, especially when we take our eye off the ball.

Fire the Assholes

The culture player has its opposite—people who are, to put it as delicately as we can, assholes.

Some time ago, we had a gifted writer who treated everyone with equal disdain. If he was on your team, you could count on both an award-winning campaign and a thoroughly miserable team experience. He was universally disliked; vengeful coworkers would head to his office whenever they had to fart.

He was no better with clients. Once, he instigated a phone fight with the president of Porsche, who "had the nerve" to suggest changes to the writer's copy. In desperation, the president said, "This conversation is gaining speed and losing altitude," and hung up. The client immediately called the account manager and said, "I don't ever want to go through that again."

This client had our trust and respect, and we were livid that anyone on our staff would treat him with such disrespect. That was the last straw. We terminated the asshole.

In the beginning, we put up with disruptive employees as long as their brilliance compensated for their negative behavior. Today, the era of the Lone Ranger genius is gone. We want top clients to talk directly with their creative teams. Open discussions lead to better work—and better working relationships. We also want *everyone* at Fallon to freely contribute ideas. If our interns have something to say, we want to hear it.

Regardless of their gifts, difficult people consume too much precious organizational energy. (Don't worry about firing them; they're talented enough to find work.) Aside from the managerial headaches, assholes hamper creative leverage. Consider BMW films. The team was dealing with Hollywood attorneys, A-list directors, and Madonna, but they pocketed their egos and pulled their weight. It's amazing what you can accomplish if you stay humble. The culture players know this. The assholes don't.

Fun Is a Competitive Advantage

Charlan Nemeth, writing in *California Management Review*, said that "desiring and expecting creativity do not necessarily increase its appearance."[2] But making your organization a more fun place to work does. Serious business writers don't want to taint their thesis with words like *fun*. But fun works. We're not just talking about socializing after work but about a quotient of fun inherent in the challenge, in the work itself.

Part of that fun must come from the interaction among team members and with clients. Team leaders and managers can't passively stand by; they must make it happen. Harvard's Teresa Amabile, a leading thinker and researcher on creativity in business culture for the past twenty years, has found that "a person's social environment can have a significant effect on that person's level of intrinsic motivation at any point in time; the level of intrinsic motivation can, in turn, have a significant effect on that person's creativity."[3]

Amabile's extensive research verifies our own experience in motivating creativity. Our primary job as organizational leaders is to cultivate the environment and provide intrinsic rewards that inspire a higher level of creativity.

Sometimes we do things for pure fun. Pat saw *Riverdance* in New York City and loved its energy. When the show came to Minneapolis, we bought out a performance for staff and families. (Pat also judges the Irish tenor contest at Murray's restaurant on St. Patrick's Day, if that helps you understand his choice of dance form.) We always look for reasons to stop and celebrate. In our very first office, we put a brass plaque on a conference table to commemorate a wonderful event: "This table was broken by Bonnie and Dan in celebration of a significant new account win."

As the leader of an organization or a team, you can use fun purposefully. Every month or so, Pat Fallon invites nineteen staffers to his house for dinner. The number is determined by the number of chairs he has, and the guest list is made up of people who Pat feels should know each other better. On several occasions, we've closed the office early to catch a movie. Pat wanted everyone to see *Schindler's List* and think about how Steven Spielberg planned this monumental film while finishing his *Indiana Jones* popcorn movie trilogy. He wanted the staff to contemplate the kind of mind that could simultaneously think about two very different projects. You'd be surprised at the number of teachable and inspirational moments that are there if you look for them.

The Future of Creative Leverage

We head into our next quarter century convinced of three things.

1. Creativity will be an increasingly essential business tool.

Think about the challenges of your own organization this way: other than creativity, what points of leverage do you have? More than likely, your resources will become more constrained, and your markets will be more hotly contested. If you can't put creativity to good use, you'll be vulnerable—to competitors from anywhere in the world. We opened this book by saying imagination was the last remaining legal means to get an edge on the competition. Increasingly, it's the only means.

2. You can't buy creativity, but you can unlock it.

Everyone draws from the same talent pool, and only the George Steinbrenners of the world have any recruiting advantage. Salary, benefits, and geographical amenities won't necessarily determine the creative power of your company. "It is easier to enhance creativity by changing conditions in the environment," writes psychologist Mihaly Csikszentmihalyi, "than by trying to make people think more creatively."[4] Rather than hire more creative people, first unleash the creativity in the people you already have on the payroll.

3. Creativity is not an easy path to walk but the rewards are worth it.

One of the heads of a rival agency in town once came up to us a local restaurant. Noting that we would get paid whether we did creative advertising or not, he joked, "Why do you have to do it the hard way?"

One reason is that we've seen the rewards, and not just with our own work. Almost every success story of the past ten years—whether it was something as brash as Apple's iPod or as unassuming as Saturn's promise for a car company you could love—has been because of creativity.

The survival of the fittest doesn't mean the survival of the strongest; it means the survival of those who are most capable of adapting to change. If you can't adapt, you can't survive. Maybe we are reflexively attracted to the hard way because we dread the alternative.

Final Thought

We have quarterly meetings where we show the entire staff new creative work. When we get lazy and skip those meeting we hear about it. What's interesting is the fact that the support staff—the accountants and IT people and human resource managers—are the first to complain. They say, "That's why we work here, too."

Creativity motivates.

We don't want to compare what we do to great works of art, but we do want to support our belief that creativity motivates all of us in powerful ways. Think about the Sydney Opera House. Not only is it an aesthetically beautiful building, there is something inspiring about the city's decision to embrace the creativity of its design. Whatever satisfaction the architects got out of dreaming up this building is matched by the satisfaction the people in the community get out of having this icon be a part of their lives. Art does as much for the audience as it does for the people who fight to bring it to life.

Chapter One

1. Purina and Fallon internal research.

2. Bob Garfield, "The Chaos Scenario," *Advertising Age,* April 4, 2005, 57.

3. Joseph Jaffe, *Life After the 30-Second Spot* (Hoboken, NJ: John Wiley & Sons, 2005), 15.

4. Motion Picture Association Worldwide Market Research, "US Entertainment Industry: 2004 MPA Market Statistics," Research Report, http://www.mpaa.org/useconomicreview/, March 2005, 29.

5. "The Consumer Advertising Backlash Worsens," Forrester Research, Inc., January 5, 2005, 3.

6. Gerald Zaltman, *How Customers Think: Essential Insights into the Mind of the Market* (Boston: Harvard Business School Press, 2003), 39.

7. "Absolut," World Advertising Research Center, brand profile, www.warc.com, December 2005, 1.

8. Robert E. Kelley, *How to Be a Star at Work* (New York: Basic Books, 1993), cited in Daniel Goleman, *Working with Emotional Intelligence* (New York: Bantam Books, 1998), 203.

9. Jeff Malester, "Best Buy Sales in U.S. Stores Increase 10%," *TWICE,* June 20, 2005, 1.

10. Karen Benezra, "Brand Planning: Youth Will Be Sold," *Brandweek,* July 14, 1997.

11. Robert J. Sternberg, Linda A. O'Hara, and Todd I. Lubart, "Creativity as Investment," *California Management Review* 40, no. 1 (1997): 16.

Chapter Two

1. "Borrowers Can Bank on More Mergers," *National Real Estate Investor*, May 2001, 8.
2. Citibank internal research.
3. David B. Hilder and Laura A. Hubbard, "Citigroup," Equity Research Report, Bear Stearns & Co, Inc., December 9, 2004, 1, from Thomson Business Intelligence, http://research.thomsonbusinessintelligence.com.
4. "Global Brands Annual Report: the Top 100 Global Brands," *BusinessWeek*, August 1, 2005, 90.
5. Citibank internal research.
6. HPI Research Group Qualitative Phase II, 2002.
7. Citibank internal research.

Chapter Three

1. Because we had no international capabilities at the time, Young & Rubicam were awarded the international portion. We were awarded the international part of the business three years later.
2. United Airlines internal research.
3. Steve Josselson, "How Low Can They Go," *Airfinance Journal*, February 1, 2003, 15.
4. United Airlines internal research.
5. *Roper Reports 02-03*, question 62X/Y, Syndicated Research, GfK NOP, LLC, 2002.
6. United's Frequent Flyer program has won numerous awards, including those listed in "Best in Business Travel Awards," *Business Traveler*, December 2004/January 2005; "Best of 2004," *Global Traveler*, December 2004/January 2005; "Awards Issue," *Travel Savvy*, September/October 2004.
7. John Tague interview with Fred Senn, November 2005.
8. Millward Brown, United Airlines Brand Health Monitor.
9. United Airlines internal research.

10. For more airline industry definitions, see the New England Regional Airport System Plan's Glossary, http://www.nerasp.com/Glossary.pdf.

11. United Airlines traffic reports.

Chapter Four

1. Millward Brown AdTracker, 2000.

2. Holiday Inn Express internal research.

3. "Marketers of the Next Generation: Jenifer Zeigler: this brand manager comforts hotel guests with extra touches in a sweet new breakfast program," *Brandweek,* April 12, 2004, 32.

4. 2004 InterContinental Hotels Investors Conference for franchisees, Chicago, September 2004.

Chapter Five

1. See, for example, "Skoda Jokes," http://web.ukonline.co.uk/members/k.frost/czech/skoda_jokes.html.

2. Victor Lewis-Smith, "Shear Class," *Daily Mirror* (London), February 26, 2000, 6.

3. Millward Brown, March 2000.

4. Randall Rothenberg, *Where Suckers Moon* (New York: Vintage Books, 1995), 128.

5. "This Week," *Daily Mirror* (London), March 28, 2000, 4.

6. Toby Young, "It's a Skoda. Honest," *Spectator* (London), October 7, 2000, 60.

7. Graham Diggines, "Brands Hatching," *Guardian* (London), April 10, 2000, 14.

8. Skoda internal research.

9. 2001 dealer satisfaction survey performed by Advantage on behalf of Skoda.

10. Skoda internal research.

11. Ibid.

12. Ken Gibson, "Motors Extra," *Sun* (London), December 22, 2000.

13. "Pick of the Month: Skoda Fabia Campaign," *Creative Review*, May 2000, 23.

14. Chris Hawken, *The Pirate Inside: Building a Challenger Brand Culture Within Yourself and Your Organization* (New York: Wiley, 2004).

Chapter Six

1. Said by an 18-year-old male in a New York City focus group conducted for Lee, 1997.

2. Judy Bloomfield, "Lee Turning to Innovation in Brand Squeeze," *WWD (Women's Wear Daily)*, October 28, 1987, 6.

3. *Denim Discussion*, Conference Program, New York City, October 19, 2005.

4. Carol Sarchet, "Buddy Lee Dolls," Minneapolis-Moline Collectors Web site, http://www.minneapolismolinecollectors.org/displays/buddy.html.

5. Ed Keller and Jon Berry, *The Influentials: One American in Ten Tells the Other Nine How to Vote, Where to Eat, and What to Buy* (New York: The Free Press, 2003), 4–8.

6. Lee internal research.

7. Members of Fallon's Lee team monitored Buddy Lee doll prices at antique shops and on eBay at the time of launch and for a few years thereafter.

8. *Lee Apparel Sales Report*, January through August 1998.

9. DRI Inc., *Lee Apparel and Advertising Tracking Study*, October 1998.

10. "Jean Therapy," *GQ*, October 2003, 228.

Chapter Seven

1. "Fact Pack," *Advertising Age*, 2005, 42.

2. Thomas Riggs, ed., *Encyclopedia of Major Marketing Campaigns* (Farmington, MI: The Gale Group, 2000), 555.

3. Kathryn Kranhold, "EDS Sends Cat Herders to the Super Bowl," *Wall Street Journal*, January 14, 2000, 1.

4. Stuart Elliott, "Big Plays, Surprise Heroes, Shocking Defeats and Other Super Bowl XXXIV Marketing Memories," *New York Times,* February 1, 2000, C10.

5. Becky Ebenkamp, "New Campaigns: Best of Show," *Brandweek,* January 31, 2000, 66.

6. Bill Breen, "How EDS Got Its Groove Back," *Fast Company,* October 2001, 106.

Chapter Eight

1. TNS Media Intelligence/CMR data cited in Jennifer Halliday, "Study Claims TV Advertising Doesn't Work on Car Buyers," *Advertising Age,* October 13, 2003, 8.

2. Automotive News Data Center, "U.S. light-vehicle sales by nameplate, December & 12 months 2005,"and "Estimated Europe light-vehicle registrations by manufacturer, November & 11 months," *Automotive News,* http://www.autonews.com/apps/pbcs.dll/section?category=datacenter02, accessed January 10, 2006.

3. Karl Greenberg, "Imports Roll On, Lower Stock in Ford, GM," *Brandweek,* June 20, 2005, S24–S25.

4. Rebecca Quick, "Victoria's Secret Causes a Big Stir With Web Blitz for 'Fashion Show,'" *Wall Street Journal,* February 4, 1999, B1.

5. BMW and Fallon internal research.

6. Jeff Green, "Instant Carma and Bad OEMs," *Brandweek,* February 7, 2000, 16–17.

7. BMW and Fallon internal research.

8. *Automotive News,* "New Car and Light Truck Sales," June 1, 2005, http://www.autonews.com.

Chapter Nine

1. Bahamas Ministry of Tourism internal data, 2004.

2. Ibid.

3. Hon. Obie Wilchcombe interview with Fred Senn, 2004.

4. Bahamas Ministry of Tourism internal data, 2004.

5. Philip Evans and Bob Wolf, "Collaboration Rules," *Harvard Business Review,* July–August 2005, 96–104.

Chapter Ten

1. United Airlines internal research.

2. Virgin Mobile and Fallon internal research, 2002.

3. Virgin Mobile's request for proposal, 2002.

4. The Intelligence Group, "April 2004 Cassandra Report," Summary, April 19, 2004, http://trendcentral.com/trends/trendarticle.asp?tcArticleId=1084.

5. Virgin Mobile internal research.

6. Virgin Mobile "Snowflakes" TV ad, 2004.

7. Virgin Mobile internal research.

8. Archipelago internal research.

9. Archipelago tracking study, wave 6, March 2003.

Chapter Eleven

1. Ed Keller and Jon Berry, *The Influentials: One American in Ten Tells the Other Nine How to Vote, Where to Eat, and What to Buy* (New York: The Free Press, 2003); and Malcolm Gladwell, *The Tipping Point: How Little Things Can Make a Difference* (Boston: Back Bay Books, 2002).

2. Charlan Jeanne Nemeth, "Managing Innovation: When Less Is More," *California Management Review* 40, no. 1 (1997): 60.

3. Teresa M. Amabile, "Motivating Creativity in Organizations: On Doing What You Love and Loving What You Do," *California Management Review* 40, no. 1 (1997): 40.

4. Mihaly Csikszentmihaly, *Creativity: Flow and the Psychology of Discovery and Invention* (New York: HarperCollins, 1996), 1.

Pat Fallon, Chairman, Fallon Worldwide

Pat founded Fallon Worldwide in 1981 with the single-minded desire for excellence—in the people hired, in the partnerships forged, in the work produced, and in the results achieved. His goal was to attract clients who wanted an aggressive marketing partnership that was broader and deeper than the traditional advertising agency relationship of the day. In creating Fallon, he wanted to build an organization in which great people came, stayed, did the best work of their careers, and had fun in the process.

Pat still spends 80 percent of his time on client business. That is why to this day Fallon limits itself to a very small group of accounts, so that he and his senior executives can be intimately involved with clients every day. He has served on senior executive committees inside *Time* magazine, Nestlé Purina, Ameritech, EDS, and United Airlines. Pat combines a deep knowledge of branding issues with a strong strategic approach to marketing problems of all kinds. He is a sought-after speaker on these issues, recently addressing the Singapore International Advertising Congress; the Asian Advertising Awards–Hong Kong; and the D&AD Conference, London's most respected advertising forum.

Pat graduated from the University of Minnesota and worked tirelessly to get the Golden Gopher football games back on campus where they belong. Thus far, he has failed.

Fred Senn, Founding Partner, Fallon Worldwide

Fred began his advertising career by managing advertising for First Bank System. Pat Fallon recruited Fred to the agency side at Martin/Williams Advertising and then asked him to be one of the founding partners of Fallon.

Today, Fred's role is less involved with account management and more involved with talent development as Fallon expands both its scope of services and its geographic reach. In this capacity, he is the Chief Learning Officer, runs Fallon University, and guest lectures at the University of Minnesota's Carlson School of Management.

A native of Minnesota, Fred is very involved in local business and nonprofit organizations. Fred has directed the successful advertising efforts of the Minnesota Business Partnership (a lobbying coalition of Minnesota companies) and the Minnesota Department of Tourism, as well as two gubernatorial campaigns. He is involved as an adviser or board member to several national children's organizations. He graduated from St. John's University and now serves on their Board of Regents.

Fred raced sports cars for ten years, but stopped suddenly in 2002. Too suddenly.

Fallon Worldwide

Fallon Worldwide, one of the world's most critically acclaimed, creatively driven branding companies, manages the consumer voice of some of the world's leading brands, including Citi, Sony, Nestlé Purina, Nordstrom, *Time* magazine, United Airlines, National Car Rental, and Alamo Rent A Car. Fallon Worldwide is a global network of Publicis Groupe, based in Paris, and has more than five hundred employees worldwide. The company has full-service offices in Minneapolis, London, Singapore, Hong Kong, São Paulo, and Tokyo. Additional information can be found at www.fallon.com.